AN INTRODUCTION TO

Index language construction

PROGRAMMED TEXTS IN
LIBRARY AND INFORMATION SCIENCE

Communication studies / K J McGarry & T W Burrell

An introduction to the Dewey decimal classification / C D Batty

An introduction to index language construction / M J Ramsden

An introduction to UDC / J M Perreault

Learn to use books & libraries / T W Burrell

Logic & Semantics in the organisation of knowledge / K J McGarry & T W Burrell

AN INTRODUCTION TO

Index language construction

A PROGRAMMED TEXT

BY

MICHAEL J RAMSDEN

BA FLA ALAA

Senior Lecturer, Department of Librarianship
Royal Melbourne Institute of Technology

LINNET BOOKS & CLIVE BINGLEY

Library of Congress Cataloging in Publication Data

Ramsden, Michael J
    An introduction to index language construction.

    (Programmed texts in library and information science)
     1. Indexing—Programmed instruction.
I. Title.

Z695.9.R35   029.5'07'7   73–19843
ISBN 0–208–01187–0

FIRST PUBLISHED 1974 BY CLIVE BINGLEY LTD
THIS EDITION SIMULTANEOUSLY PUBLISHED IN THE USA BY
LINNET BOOKS, AN IMPRINT OF THE SHOE STRING PRESS, INC,
995 SHERMAN AVENUE, HAMDEN, CONNECTICUT 06514
PRINTED IN GREAT BRITAIN
© MICHAEL J RAMSDEN 1974
ALL RIGHTS RESERVED

AUTHOR'S NOTE

THIS BOOK HAS GROWN out of an exercise devised for use in teaching the theory of classification at the College of Librarianship Wales, and I am indebted to David Batty for the suggestion that it be developed into a programmed text, and for encouraging me to undertake the work. I must also acknowledge a debt to the students in Wales with whom I used the exercise, and whose comments helped to refine my ideas, and to the students of LI 322 in the Department of Librarianship at the Royal Melbourne Institute of Technology in 1972 with whom I worked through the programme; the experience gained then, and their comments, resulted in a number of important improvements to the text. I should also like to acknowledge the help of colleagues and friends in Wales and Australia, and especially Elaine Roache and John Horner, whose comments on the text were most helpful. Not least, I acknowledge with gratitude the help and encouragement of my wife, without whom the book would never have been completed, and as a final word I should like to record my very great debt to Jack Mills, an inspiring teacher, who first fired my interest in subject indexing when I was a student at what was then the North-Western Polytechnic School of Librarianship. He it was who taught me the importance of clear and unambiguous subject analysis.

INTRODUCTION

THIS BOOK IS INTENDED to provide instruction in the rudiments of index language construction. After instructing you in basic subject analysis, it aims to show how that analysis may be manipulated to arrive at *either* a classification scheme, *or* an alphabetical list of subject headings, *or* a thesaurus. It is possible to use the book to study the rudiments of the construction of any one of the three, or of all of them.

The book is not intended to be read as a conventional textbook, and its 'pages' are not numbered as pages. Each 'page' represents a frame which is concerned with a single point of instruction. At the foot of each frame you are directed to which frame you should turn next. At the foot of some frames you will find a question on the information you have been given in the frame just completed, and you will be offered a number of solutions, only one of which is correct. If you choose the correct answer you will be directed to the next stage of instruction; if you choose an incorrect answer you will be guided to an intermediate frame where you will be shown your mistake and given further instruction, before being asked a further question which gives you the opportunity of reaching the next main step in the course. If at any time you wish to consult a particular part of the programme you may do this by using the *Concept index* facing this page.

You may now turn over to frame 1 and begin.

CONCEPT INDEX

Frame

BT notes	195
Categories: Recognition	30
Characteristics of division	30
Combination order	71
Common categories	41
Compound concepts	6
Fundamental categories	41
Index languages	1
NT notes	190
Natural language indexing	1
Notation	121
Order within categories	113
Post-coordinate index languages	174
Pre-coordinate index languages	69
Principle of inversion	106
Properties category	28
RT notes	200
References: construction	136
See also references	153
See references	128
Sub-categories	62
USED FOR notes	189
USE instructions	181
x instructions	126
xx instructions	157

1 All spoken languages consist of two basic elements: a vocabulary, and a grammatical structure (syntax). Writers on information retrieval often use the term *natural language* to denote spoken languages. It is possible, in indexing, to employ natural language, that is to use language simply as it is spoken, or used in documents. without attempting, for example, to control synonyms (by consistently adopting one rather than another), or to indicate the relationships between terms. Such an index is often referred to as a *natural language index*.

The alternative to natural language indexing is to use an artificial language adapted to our needs, *ie* an *index language*. Such a language will reflect a controlled vocabulary, that is to say that careful decisions will have been made as to the terms to be used and the meaning to be attached to each.

What do you understand by an index language?

After answering this question turn to frame 2.

2 You should have answered that an index language is an artificial language which is adapted to the requirements of indexing. The vocabulary of an index language will be controlled. If your answer was not in these, or similar, terms, you should re-read frame 1 before proceeding.

An index language may also seek to indicate the relationships between the terms in its vocabulary. For example if our system includes the terms *Secondary education* and *Independent schools* then we might seek to indicate the relationship between these two terms, since a user seeking information on *Secondary education* and referring to that term in the index, might also find relevant information under the other term—*Independent schools*, since these schools usually provide education at the secondary level. An index language which has a controlled vocabulary, and which attempts to indicate the relationships between terms in the index vocabulary, is said to be *structured*.

There are various kinds of structured index language, classification schemes being only one, if perhaps the most familiar, example. Sears *List of subject headings* is an example of a second kind, the Engineers Joint Council *Thesaurus of engineering and scientific terms* an example of a third kind.

It is the purpose of this programme to teach a method for compiling a structured index language of each of these basic kinds, and in doing so to bring out the principles and features which are common to all of them as well as those which are distinctive to each.

What do you understand by a *structured* index language?

When you have answered this question turn to frame 3.

3 You should have answered that a structured index language is one which not only has a controlled vocabulary, but which also seeks to indicate the relationships between terms. If your answer was not substantially in these terms re-read frame 2 before proceeding.

All structured index languages consist of:
a) a vocabulary
b) a syntax.

The *vocabulary* is the list of terms used in the system. The vocabulary of the system will be smaller than that of the users of the system, smaller than that used in the documents which will be indexed by the system, and smaller than that used by the indexer himself. This situation arises from the control of the vocabulary as described in frame 1. Because of this we shall need to provide, in addition to an index vocabulary (the terms used in the index), an *approach vocabulary* consisting of terms which are not used in the index but which might be used by users, writers or indexers, especially by users in preparing to search the index.

The *syntax* is the pattern of relationships which we recognize between the terms used in the system, *ie* between the terms in the index vocabulary. This recognition is based upon a careful subject analysis which is basic to all structured index languages.

What are the essential features of a structured index language?

Turn to frame 5.

4 You should have answered to the effect that the essential features of a structured index language are a vocabulary and a syntax, and that in addition to the index vocabulary (the terms used in the system) we need to provide an approach vocabulary (terms not used in the system but which might be used by users and others). If your answer did not cover these points you should read again through frame 3 before proceeding.

The vocabulary of an index language may be *verbal* or *coded*. A classification scheme employs a coded vocabulary in the form of its notation. Thus in the *Dewey Decimal Classification* ' British History ' is rendered as 942; in Sears *List of subject headings* however, which employs a verbal vocabulary, it is rendered as Great Britain—History. But whichever kind of vocabulary we anticipate using the first step in constructing our index vocabulary will be to select the terms to be used, the coding, if necessary, is a much later stage.

There are a number of possible ways by which we might select our terms. We might rely on our knowledge of the subject to suggest relevant terms, or we might consult others more expert than ourselves, or we might do both. Alternatively we might consult published classification schemes, or thesauri of indexing terms. Much the most useful and reliable source, however, would be the literature of the subject which the system will be designed to handle; we should, therefore, examine the literature, in order to establish the terms used by those writing and practising in the field, and any other source should be strictly ancillary. An index language whose vocabulary is thus based may be said to possess *literary warrant*.

How should we select the terms to be used in our indexing system?

When you have answered this question turn to frame 5.

5 The selection of terms to be used in our indexing system should be based primarily on a survey of the literature. If your answer was not in these terms re-read frame 4 before proceeding.

If we examine the literature of EDUCATION we might find, amongst many others, the following titles/phrases/subjects:—

1 The condition of state schools in Scotland in the 19th century
2 The overhead projector: a new teaching aid
3 Science in the primary school
4 Roman Catholic schools in Ulster
5 A survey of the information provided in University prospectuses
6 Comprehensive schools[1] in the United Kingdom
7 Standards of book provision in secondary school libraries
8 Adult education and anthropology
9 Television in the primary school
10 The use of film-strips in elementary chemistry
11 Climbing frames in school playgrounds
12 Domestic science for girls in primary schools
13 The education of children from areas of slum housing
14 Higher education in the United States during the 1930's
15 Sport in the public schools in England
16 Teaching reading to children with dyslexia
17 Recruitment of graduate teachers for primary schools
18 Programmed learning for the blind
19 Research into the use of video tape in the education of mentally handicapped children
20 Teaching English to immigrant children in Australia
21 Physical education for physically handicapped children
22 Advanced level history: a curriculum for part-time students
23 Social science in the polytechnics[2]
24 The problem of vocabulary in the popularisation of science
25 A comparison of the attitudes to education of working class children and middle class children

Turn now to frame 6.

Notes
1 Non-selective schools
2 Institutions of tertiary education of non-university status

6 The examination of the literature reveals the basic terminology of the subject. We shall need to decide which terms to adopt as our index vocabulary, and which to include in the approach vocabulary, but it will be easier to defer this decision until we have completed our subject analysis, since at that stage the terms in question (*eg* synonyms) will be more easily identifiable.

However, before we proceed further we should examine our terms to ensure that each one represents a single concept only. For example, *Scotland* in item 1 represents the single concept of the geo-political area which bears that name; on the other hand, in an index language for the subject of Building the term *bungalow* (in British usage) represents a compound concept of a *single storey* building for *residential use*. We can put this another way and say that whereas *Scotland* reflects only one idea (geo-political place) *bungalow* reflects two (Building by number of storeys, and building by use). In an index language the single term would be used in the approach vocabulary, whilst in the index vocabulary the separate terms would be used.

In item 12 in frame 5 one of the terms represents a compound concept which can be expressed by two separate terms. Identify the term in question.

Domestic science—turn to frame 16.

Girls—turn to frame 48.

Primary—turn to frame 8.

7 No, you have made the same mistake again.

It seems obvious that *elementary* reflects the characteristic of level, and so indeed it does. But we are concerned at this stage with establishing broad categories, and in order to identify accurately the broadest category to which a term belongs we must be prepared to look beyond the obvious. In the broadest sense *elementary* is a question of the level at which we teach the contents of a curriculum, and thus the broad category to which the term belongs is **Curriculum**. Similarly *science* is a subject in a curriculum, and so it too belongs to the broad category of **Curriculum**.

It is important to identify the broadest category since failure to do so will obscure relationships. Thus, if we do not recognize that **Subjects** and **Levels** each belong to the broader **Curriculum** category, the result will be that our index language will not highlight the relationship between the subjects in a curriculum and the level at which they are taught.

Turn now to frame 46.

---

8 No.

Primary reflects only the single concept of a particular stage of education. What we are looking for is a term which is defined by two different concepts. In the previous frame you were given the example of *bungalow* (in British usage); another example is *convent* which reflects no less than three concepts—a *residential* building used by *female* members of a *religious* order.

Consider the following title:

The education of women in England during the Middle Ages.

Which of the terms in this title represents a compound concept?

Women—turn to frame 26.

England—turn to frame 34.

Middle Ages—turn to frame 38.

9 No.

We must always select the essential characteristic, and the decision as to what is the essential characteristic must always be made in the context of the subject. The role of a library in education is not that of a building (the library would still be a library if it were accommodated in cupboards in a classroom), and this is not an index language for Architecture. If the issue is not clear examine our list in frame 5 and see what other terms you think should be in the same category as *libraries*.

What characteristic is reflected by *playgrounds* in item 11?

Facilities—turn to frame 13.

Recreation areas—turn to frame 24.

---

10 No.

A moment's thought will demonstrate that *Past* cannot be the characteristic for which you are looking. Clearly *20th century* (and even *21st century*) are terms related to *19th century*, but they do not as yet belong to the past; the one may be regarded as present, the other clearly is *future*. In fact, *past, present* and *future* are terms which belong to the same category as *19th century* etc. All are temporal concepts, and the characteristic which they reflect is Time. They belong to the **Time** category.

Now turn to frame 37.

---

11 No.

It is not an essential characteristic of *provision* that it is a problem, indeed it need not necessarily be so. The essential characteristic of *provision* is that it is an **Operation**.

Now turn to frame 28.

---

12 No.

This category would be too narrow. Certainly *state schools* does specify schools by ownership (*ie* schools owned by, or organized and financed by, the state). But if we recognize this as the broad category we shall obscure the relationship with schools specified by some other characteristic.

For example, what characteristic is reflected by *comprehensive schools* in item 6?

Schools—turn to frame 15.

Basis of selection—turn to frame 78.

13 Right.

There are now 4 further categories to identify.

What characteristic is reflected by *programmed learning* in item 18?

Operations—turn to frame 39.

Teaching and learning methods—turn to frame 23.

---

14 The distinction between the **Schools** category and the **Educands** category is sometimes not immediately apparent, and we shall need to exercise care in allocating terms between these two categories.

To which category does *Polytechnics* belong?

Educands—turn to frame 52.

Schools—turn to frame 43.

---

15 Quite right.

Notice that *state schools* belongs to the same broad category, and that your failure to realize this, if uncorrected, would have obscured the relationship between *state schools* (schools specified by one characteristic) and *comprehensive schools* (schools specified by another characteristic).

Turn now to frame 25.

---

16 No.

Domestic science is an example of a single concept represented by two words. The only concept involved is that of the subject in a school curriculum which we call 'Domestic science'. What we are looking for is a single term which reflects two linked concepts. In the previous frame you were given the example of *bungalow* (in British usage); another example is *convent* which reflects no less than three concepts—a *residential* building used by *female* members of a *religious* order.

Consider the following title:

The education of women in England during the Middle Ages.

Which of the terms in this title represents a compound concept?

Women—turn to frame 26.

England—turn to frame 34.

Middle Ages—turn to frame 38.

17 Quite right.

Place is the broad characteristic which governs the grouping of terms such as *Scotland, Ulster, United States* etc. into a **Place** category.

A Place category will occur in any subject, since any subject may be qualified by reference to a particular area (*eg* Science *in Britain*; Labour relations *in Australia*; Art *in the United States*; Industrial development *in India*). Categories which can be identified in any subject area are termed *common categories*; **Place** is one of three. We will next identify the other two.

What characteristic is reflected by *19th century* in item 1 in frame 5?

Past—turn to frame 10.

Period, Time, or similar terms—turn to frame 37.

---

18 You should have answered that *common categories* include the same terms in any subject, whereas *fundamental categories* may include different terms in some subjects, even though the idea governing the grouping (the characteristic of division) may be the same. If your answer was along these lines please turn to frame 73. If, however, your answer was different, or if you were uncertain of the answer, read on.

Common categories are so called because not only does the characteristic occur in all subjects, but it also produces the same terms in all subjects. Thus *Great Britain* will occur in the place category for any subject (Christianity in *Britain* today; Traffic problems in *Britain;* Family relationships in *Britain,* etc). However, it does not always follow that the same characteristic, applied in different subject areas, will result in the same group of terms. Thus in AGRICULTURE, the **Operations** category will comprise terms such as *Ploughing, Harvesting, Sowing,* etc, whereas in ENGINEER-ING the terms will be different—*Welding, Drilling, Reaming,* etc. Categories which include different terms in different subjects will be referred to as *fundamental categories*.

Now turn to frame 19.

19 We can now turn to our list in frame 5 and see whether we can identify any terms as belonging to a fundamental category.

We should remember that at this stage we are concerned with broad categories, and that in identifying the category to which a term belongs we are looking for the broadest category where there appears to be two or more alternatives.

What characteristic is reflected by *overhead projectors* in item 2?

Teaching aids—turn to frame 27.

Equipment—turn to frame 33.

---

20 Quite right.

To recapitulate, we have so far identified:

3 common categories—**Place**; **Time**; **Common subdivisions**.

4 fundamental categories—**Equipment**; **Agents**; **Operations**; **Properties**.

There are a number of categories yet to be identified, most of them peculiar to Education. We will, therefore, continue to examine the terms in the subject.

What characteristic is reflected by *libraries* in item 7?

Buildings (*ie* parts of schools)—turn to frame 9.

Facilities—turn to frame 13.

---

21 No.

Certainly *graduate* does belong to a qualifications sub-category, but remember that we are concerned at this stage with broad categories. **Qualifications** itself belongs to a broader category of **Properties**, and it is to this broader category that *graduate* should be assigned at this stage.

Consider the title *Recruitment of married women to the teaching profession*.

What characteristic is reflected by *married*?

Properties—turn to frame 20.

Marital status—turn to frame 31.

22 No.

It seemed that you had grasped the point at issue, but evidently it is not yet wholly clear. Primary represents the single concept of a stage of education, whereas we are looking for a compound concept.

Go back to frame 6 and work through it again carefully before attempting the question at the foot of the frame.

---

23 Good.

You will probably have noticed, from your experience so far, that some categories are more readily identified than others. You should, however, always check carefully, and not jump to conclusions just because the solution seems obvious.

What characteristic is reflected by *science* in item 3?

Subjects—turn to frame 42.

Curriculum—turn to frame 46.

---

24 No.

You have not selected the broadest category. *Playgrounds* may certainly be said to belong to a category of **Recreation areas,** which would also include terms (not in our sample list) such as *playing fields, squash courts,* etc. But the category of Recreation areas is itself part of a wider category of **Facilities.** It is important that you understand the importance of choosing the widest possible category.

Read frame 27 and then turn to frame 20 and work through this phase of the programme again.

---

25 Good.

We will prefer **Schools** to Institutions as the name of the category, since the former is the more comprehensive term.

This category was relatively easy to identify, the problem lies in identifying our final category and establishing its scope and its relationship to our **Institutions** category.

What characteristic is reflected by *primary* in item 3?

Stage of education—turn to frame 35.

Educands—turn to frame 40.

Schools—turn to frame 44.

26 Good, you are rght.

Women reflects the two concepts of person by age (adult) and person by sex (female), *ie* women = adult females.

Now that you have grasped the idea look again at item 12 in frame 5. Which term reflects two concepts?

Domestic science—turn to frame 45.

Girls—turn to frame 48.

Primary—turn to frame 22.

---

27 No, this places the term in too narrow a category.

A structured index language should seek to reflect, or display, all the significant relationships between the terms in its index vocabulary. Any given term may be in a hierarchical relationship with other terms, for example: Building materials—Timber—Hardwoods—Teak. If, in an index language for BUILDING, we assigned *Teak* to a category of **Hardwoods**, we should obscure its relationship to *Timber*, and to any kind of timber (*eg softwoods*) which would not belong to the sub-category of **Hardwoods**. Similarly, if we assign *overhead projectors*, at this stage, to a category of **Teaching aids**, we should obscure the relationship between overhead projectors and any item of equipment which is not a teaching aid. At this early stage, therefore, we should assign *overhead projectors* to the wider category of **Equipment**.

What characteristic is reflected by film-strips in item 10?

Audio-visual aids—turn to frame 75.

Equipment—turn to frame 33.

28 Good.

We have now identified all but one of the fundamental categories in our subject. The one remaining is a **Properties** category.

There are certain problems in accurately identifying a **Properties** category. Any characteristic which we identify is, by definition, a property of the terms or concepts included in the resulting category. For example, it is a property of the terms included in the **Agents** category that they all represent the concept of a person who performs some operation, *ie,* they possess the property of being agents. This is a truism. Here is a problem when we seek to identify a **Properties** category; unless we exercise careful control we shall end by including in it all the terms in our index vocabulary. In the sense that a characteristic adopted as the basis of a category, *ie* as its ruling characteristic, may be regarded as a property, it is associated only with the terms within that category: that other terms do not possess the characteristic is the basis for their exclusion. However, for the terms which are included within the category it is a necessary and essential characteristic. A **Properties** category should include only those terms which are not associated exclusively with one category, and are not, therefore, a property of one category only. Thus *Handicap* is, in EDUCATION, only associated with students who, as we shall see, form a separate category, consequently *Handicap* is not included within the **Properties** category but is associated with students; on the other hand *part-time* might be associated with the Educands category (part-time students) or with agents (part-time teachers), so part-time belongs in the **Properties** category.

What characteristic is reflected by *graduate* in title 17?

Agents—turn to frame 67.

Properties—turn to frame 20.

Qualifications—turn to frame 21.

29 No, you are quite wrong.

Elementary is in no sense a method of teaching. We may employ various methods in teaching subjects at an elementary level— programmed learning, demonstration, lectures, etc, but *elementary* remains a matter of level and a curriculum question. Because we are concerned to establish broad categories we have to decide whether **Curriculum** or **Level** is the broader category.

To which category should *elementary* be assigned in our initial analysis?

Curriculum—turn to frame 46.

Level—turn to frame 7.

30 The syntax in an index language is essentially a question of the recognition of certain relationships between the terms in the language, or, more precisely, the recognition of the relationships between the concepts represented by those terms. Subject analysis, in index language construction, is the process by which we establish the relationships to be recognized, and it underlies any structured index language since it is an essential feature of such a language that it seeks to display relationships.

The first step in this subject analysis is a grouping process by which we seek to group together terms which share an essential relationship. This is a process with which most people are familiar, it underlies the very language by which we communicate. For example, when we use the word *criminals* we understand that we are referring to all those people who share the essential common characteristic of having offended against the criminal law. Furthermore, bank robbers, forgers, murderers, blackmailers, and kidnappers are all understood to be kinds of criminal (*ie* to belong to that group, or *class*) because they, too, possess the essential characteristic. The use of the word 'essential' is important and should be noted carefully. Any person or object will possess several characteristics, but the one we select as the principle to govern our grouping process will be that which is essential to our purpose. So, for example, in grouping persons for the purpose of criminology, we ignore the fact that they may be dark or fair, or tall or short; we note only whether or not they have offended against the criminal law.

This is a classificatory process (the groups are, in fact, classes), and it can eventually lead to the production of a classification scheme. However, it is a process which is basic to *any* structured index language. At this stage its purpose is not to produce a classification, but to establish relationships which a structured index language should display.

What is the first step in subject analysis, and why is it important?

When you have answered this question turn to frame 50.

31 No.

You have made the same mistake again, for marital status is itself part of a wider **Properties** category. It is of the greatest importance that in the initial stage of our subject analysis we identify the broad categories, leaving the more detailed analysis until later.

To ensure that you understand this point read frame 27, and then go to frame 28 and work through this phase of the programme again.

---

32 No, you are wrong.

The United Kingdom, or Great Britain, is not a characteristic, nor is the relationship of *Scotland* to either of them that of a concept to a characteristic. Scotland is part of Great Britain and a part of the United Kingdom, and clearly a concept cannot be a part of a characteristic which it possesses.

If we examine the list of terms we see that, for example, the *United States* in item 14 reflects the same characteristic as *Scotland*. On further consideration, therefore, what characteristic is reflected by the terms *Scotland* and the *United States*.

Geo-political place, or Country—turn to frame 49.
Place—turn to frame 17.

---

33 Good, you are quite right.

The most general category to which *overhead projectors,* and also *film-strips* (in item 10), belongs is **Equipment**. Each belongs also to a category of **Teaching aids**, and to a yet narrower category of **Audio-visual aids**. However, at this stage we are concerned with the broadest category, which you have correctly identified as being **Equipment**.

This is one of the fundamental categories which may be identified in our subject. There are others.

What characteristic is reflected by *Teachers* in item 17?

Agents—turn to frame 74.
Persons—turn to frame 36.

34 No.

You have not yet grasped the idea. England represents the single concept of geo-political place, whereas we are looking for a term which reflects two concepts.

Go back to frame 6 and work through it again carefully before attempting the question at the foot of the frame.

---

35 No.

Your solution places primary in too narrow a category. You should have grasped by now that we are concerned with broad categories. It is quite true that the distinguishing characteristic of primary education is that it is provided to persons who are at the primary stage of their education. This states the characteristic precisely, but this will eventually be a sub-category within a broader category, and it is with the broader category that we are concerned at present. Consider the question again.

What characteristic is reflected by *primary* in item 3?

Educands—turn to frame 40.

Schools—turn to frame 44.

---

36 No.

Remember that we must select the *essential* characteristic. It is not essential to the definition of teachers that they are people, so indeed are their pupils, yet the latter do not belong to the same category as teachers. The essential characteristic of teachers is that they perform an operation—that of teaching. Teachers, therefore, belongs to a category of persons who perform an operation, *ie* to the category of **Agents**.

Now turn to frame 74.

37 Good.

Time, like **Place**, is a common category. The other common category is usually called **Common subdivisions**. This category accommodates terms which denote either the physical form in which information is presented, *eg* a *periodical* or a *dictionary* (Common subdivisions of form), or the point of view from which the subject is treated, *eg* a *bibliography* of science, or a *history* of education (Common subject divisions). Common subdivisions of form do not limit subject coverage in any way, a periodical dealing with Education could cover any aspect of the subject; common subject divisions, on the other hand, do limit subject coverage, a History of Education would treat of the subject from that point of view only.

What is the third common category, besides **Place** and **Time**? What does it include?

When you have answered this question turn to frame 41.

---

38 No.

You have not yet grasped the idea. Middle Ages is a single concept—a particular historical period—represented by two words, whereas we are looking for a single word which represents a compound concept.

Go back to frame 6 and work through it again carefully before attempting the question at the foot of the frame.

---

39 No.

Programmed learning is not so much something done (Operation) as a way of carrying out a particular operation, that of teaching. It is, therefore, essentially a method—a method of teaching, and of learning. The essential characteristic, and thus the category to which we should assign it, is **Teaching and learning methods**.

Turn now to frame 23.

40 Very good.

You are quite right, although in fact, as you may have noticed, the decision is not an easy one to reach. One of the leading index languages in the field, D J Foskett's *London Education Classification*,[1] has in fact not made the distinction, opting instead for a combined **Schools and Educands** category.

The basis of the distinction we are making in this programme is that the distinguishing characteristic of a primary school, or a secondary school, or a tertiary institution (or an institution of higher education), lies in the fact that the students (*ie* Educands) are at a particular stage of their education. Moreover, the literature on primary education, secondary education, etc is, on the whole, concerned with the pupils rather than with the institutions *per se*. In other words a primary school is distinguished by a characteristic of its pupils (*ie* Educands).

Notice that the **Educands** category will be quite extensive, and will include a number of sub-categories.

Now turn to frame 14.

1 Foskett, D J: *London Education Classification, Education libraries bulletin*, Supplement 6, 1963.

41 You should have replied that the third common category is **Common subdivisions**, and that it comprises common form divisions (which designate the physical form in which information is presented), and common subject divisions (which designate the point of view from which the subject is treated). If you did not answer to this effect re-read frame 70 before proceeding.

The categories of **Place**, **Time**, and **Common subdivisions** are referred to as *common categories* because they occur in all subjects and always include the same terms. However, some theorists have developed the idea that it may be possible to establish certain *fundamental categories* which will occur in most, if not all, subjects, without necessarily producing the same terms. (As usually developed fundamental categories would include common categories, at least place and time. However, the idea will be used in this text as excluding the three common categories, and it is considered that the distinction is useful.) A fairly obvious fundamental category would be **Things**, which in AGRICULTURE would comprise Crops, and in CHEMISTRY elements and chemical compounds. E J Coates has recognized **Thing**, **Part**, **Material**, **Action** (Operation) and **Property**;[1] we can add to these **Agent** (*ie* persons or substances performing or used in an operation) and **Equipment**.

What distinction have we made between *common categories* and fundamental categories?

When you have answered this question please turn to frame 18.

1 Coates, E J: *Subject catalogues: headings and structure*. Library Association, 1960, Chapter 6.

42 No, you have jumped to the wrong conclusion.

The answer *subjects* seems obvious, but unfortunately it is only half-correct. *Science* is, of course, one of the subjects which may be taught in schools, but subjects is not the widest category to which the term belongs, being itself part of a wider category.

Try another example.

What characteristic is reflected by *elementary* in item 10?

Level—turn to frame 7.

Curriculum—turn to frame 46.

Teaching methods—turn to frame 29.

---

43 No.

Remember that the distinction between the **Schools** category on the one hand and the **Educands** category on the other, lay in the fact that the distinguishing characteristic of terms in the latter category was in the students. In the case of *polytechnics* the distinguishing feature lies in the fact that the students are at the tertiary stage of their education. Accordingly *polytechnics* should be allocated to the **Educands** category.

Try another example.

The magazine of the Yarra Valley Church of England school.
To which category should *Church of England* be allocated?

Schools—turn to frame 52.

Educands—turn to frame 47.

44 Not quite.

The characteristic which distinguishes a primary school is the fact that its pupils are at a particular stage of their education, and similarly with a secondary school, and with the various kinds of tertiary institution (or institutions of higher education). Moreover, the literature on primary education, secondary education, etc is, on the whole, concerned with the pupils rather than with the institutions *per se*. In other words a primary school is distinguished by a characteristic of its pupils (*ie* Educands). It would seem, therefore, that *primary* should be placed in an **Educands** category.

Thus we have decided to distinguish between a **Schools** category and an **Educands** category. The reasons for this decision are set out above, but the decision is not without its difficulties in practice (though this programme endeavours to use examples which avoid the worst problems). It should be noted also that one of the leading index languages in the field, D J Foskett's *London Education Classification*, deliberately does not make the distinction, opting instead for a combined **Schools and Educands** category.

Notice that our Educands category will be quite extensive, and will include a number of sub-categories.

Now turn to frame 14.

1 Foskett, D J: *London Education Classification, Education libraries bulletin,* Supplement 6, 1963.

45 No.

It seemed that you had grasped the point at issue, but it is evidently not wholly clear yet. Domestic science is an example of a single concept—the subject in a school curriculum which we call by that name—which is represented by two words. We, however, are looking for a single word which represents a compound concept.

Go back to frame 6 and work through it again carefully before attempting the question at the foot of the frame.

---

46 Good.

We are approaching the end of our initial subject analysis into broad categories, but there remain the two most difficult categories.

The difficulty will lie mainly in distinguishing between them, but we will probably be able to agree without too much difficulty as to the identity of the first.

What characteristic is reflected by *state schools* in item 3?

Schools, or Institutions—turn to frame 25.

Ownership—turn to frame 12.

---

47 No. I am afraid you are wrong again.

The distinguishing characteristic in this case does not lie in the students, but in the school and in its ownership. Consequently *Church of England* should be allocated to the **Schools** category.

To make sure that you have grasped the distinction between the two categories work through frame 40 again, and proceed from there.

48 Quite right.

Girls reflects two concepts, namely person by age (children) and person by sex (female), *ie Girls* = Female children. Since in our analysis we shall wish to deal only in simple concepts, we shall use the terms *children* and *female* in the index vocabulary, whilst *girls* will feature in the approach vocabulary.

The remaining question in connection with our vocabulary, that of deciding which of the terms in the list in frame 5 shall be included in the index vocabulary, and which in the approach vocabulary, we have decided to defer to a later stage. We may note, however, that the majority of terms will be included in the index vocabulary. The need for a choice between index vocabulary and approach vocabulary will arise only in the case of synonyms (or near synonyms) and antonyms.

We can now, therefore, consider the question of syntax, or the relationships between terms. Please turn to frame 30.

49 Not quite.

Certainly, the precise characteristic reflected by *Scotland* is geo-political place. But at this stage we are concerned with broad characteristics, in order to arrive at broad categories, and geo-political place (or country) defines the category too closely. The *broad* category is **Place,** and at a later stage we shall define certain sub-groupings, or sub-categories, one of which will be geo-political place.

A place category can be identified in any subject, since any subject can be qualified by reference to a particular area (*eg* Science *in Britain*; Labour relations *in Australia*; Art in the *United States*; Industrial development *in India*). Moreover, it will clearly always include the same terms. Categories which can be identified in any subject, and which always include the same terms, are termed *common categories*; **Place** is one of three. We will next identify the other two.

What characteristic is reflected by *19th century* in item 1 in frame 5?

Past—turn to frame 10.

Period, Time, or similar terms—turn to frame 37.

50 You should have answered that the first step in subject analysis is a grouping process which is important because its purpose is to establish the relationships which a structured index language should display. If your answer was not substantially along these lines you should work through frame 30 again before proceeding.

The grouping process, in index language construction, seeks to assemble our terms into broad categories, and we proceed along the lines indicated in the previous frame. That is, we examine each term and ask ourselves what is the essential characteristic which it reflects. For example, if we were dealing with the subject of CLOTHING, *cotton* reflects the essential characteristic of *material, ie cotton* is a term in the class *material*. In classificatory terms this is referred to as division, since the terms within the subject, or basic class, are divided into a number of categories (or classes). The characteristics which govern the division are known as characteristics of division. If it is not clear what characteristic a particular term reflects, the question can usually be resolved by seeking other terms which appear to be related, and then identifying the essential characteristic which they share.

What do you understand by a *characteristic of division*? When you have answered this question turn to frame 51.

51 You should have answered that a characteristic of division is the idea which governs our grouping of terms into a category. If your answer was not along these lines re-read frame 50 before proceeding.

It is important to bear in mind that, at this early stage, we are assembling broad categories. If our initial categories are drawn too narrowly we shall obscure relationships. For example, in CLOTHING, *hats* should be placed initially in the broad category of *wearing apparel*, not in the category of *headgear* which would obscure the relationship between hats and items worn elsewhere, such as *gloves* or *scarves*.

Bearing this in mind we can now embark on our subject analysis by examining our sample terms. You will find it convenient to fold out frame 5 for easy reference.

Looking at the list in frame 5, what characteristic is reflected by *Scotland*?

United Kingdom, Great Britain, or similar—turn to frame 32.

Country, or Geo-political place—turn to frame 49.

Place—turn to frame 17.

52 Good, you are quite right.

If we examine the remaining terms in our list we shall find that the characteristic reflected by each is one already identified: we have now identified all the broad characteristics in our subject. The complete list, in the order in which we identified them, is:

Place
Time
Common subdivisions
Equipment
Agents
Operations
Properties
Facilities
Teaching and learning methods
Curriculum
Schools
Educands

At this stage the order of the categories has absolutely no significance, the order is simply the random order in which we identified the various characteristics and the resulting categories.

The next stage in our analysis will be to allocate each of the terms in our list to one of the above categories. Remember that at this stage the categories are relatively broad; they may be subdivided at a later stage.

As the order of categories has no importance at this stage it will be most convenient to take each category in turn, in the order in which they appear above.

Allocate terms from the list in frame 5 to the **Place** category, and then turn to frame 53.

53 The **Place** category comprises:

Scotland; Ulster; United Kingdom; Areas of slum housing; United States; England; Australia

Perhaps the apearance of *Areas of slum housing* in this list will occasion surprise; but remember that our categories are relatively broad at this stage, and may be capable of further subdivision. **Place,** therefore, need not equate with geo-political place. If we speak of schools in areas of slum housing, we are referring to schools in a particular kind of area, even though the area may be characterized in a way other than by its geo-political affiliation.

Now allocate terms from our list to the **Time** category, and then to the **Common subdivisions** category. When you have done this turn to frame 54.

---

54 The **Time** category is fairly straightforward and includes only:

19th century; 1930's

The **Common subdivisions** category comprises:

Prospectuses; Standards; Vocabulary

Now allocate terms to the **Equipment** category, and then to the **Agents** category. Then turn to frame 55.

---

55 The **Equipment** category comprises:

Overhead projectors; Teaching aids; Books; Television; Filmstrips; Climbing frames; Video tape

The **Agents** category comprises:

Teachers; Home environment

Now allocate terms to the **Operations** category, and then to the **Properties** category. Then turn to frame 56.

---

56 The **Operations** category comprises:

Provision; Teaching; Recruitment

The **Properties** category comprises:

Graduate; Part-time

Now allocate terms to the **Facilities** category, and then to the **Teaching methods** category. Then turn to frame 57.

57 The **Facilities** category comprises:
Libraries; Playgrounds
The **Teaching methods** category comprises:
Programmed learning; Popularization
We have now three categories remaining to which terms have not been allocated, but we have allocated only about half the terms in our list. This is because two of the remaining categories are relatively extensive.

Allocate terms to the **Curriculum** category, and then turn to frame 58.

---

58 The **Curriculum** category comprises:
Science; Anthropology; Elementary; Chemistry; Domestic science; Sport; Reading; English; Physical education; Advanced; History; Social sciences

Now allocate terms to the **Schools** category. In doing so bear in mind the distinction between it and the **Educands** category. In the latter the governing characteristic is inherent in the Educand, in the former it is inherent in the Institution itself.

When you have allocated terms to the **Schools** category turn to frame 59.

---

59 The **Schools** category comprises:
Roman Catholic; Comprehensive; Public; State

Now, finally, allocate terms to the **Educands** category. Then turn to frame 60.

---

60 The **Educands** category comprises the remaining significant terms, viz:
Primary; University; Secondary; Adults; Children; Females; Higher; Dyslexia; Mentally handicapped; Immigrants; Blind; Physically handicapped; Students; Polytechnics; Working class; Middle class

Now turn to frame 61.

61 The complete analysis of the basic categories is as follows. Note that in some cases terms have been added to those derived from our sample list in frame 5, the better to demonstrate the scope of the various categories.

Place
Scotland; Ulster; United Kingdom; Areas of slum housing; United States; England; Australia; Wales; Rural; Victoria; Urban; South Australia

Time
19th century; 1930's; 18th century; 1970's; 20th century

Common subdivisions
Prospectuses; Standards; Vocabulary; Periodicals; Research

Equipment
Overhead projectors; Teaching aids; Books; Television; Filmstrips; Climbing frames; Video tapes; Desks; Chairs

Agents
Teachers; Home environment; Inspectors; Parents

Operations
Provision; Teaching; Recruitment; Purchase; Promotion

Properties
Graduate; Part-time; Married; Full-time; Non-graduate

Facilities
Libraries; Playgrounds; Laboratories; Classrooms

Teaching methods
Programmed learning; Popularization

Curriculum
Science; Anthropology; Elementary; Chemistry; Domestic science; Sport; Reading; English language; English literature; Physical education; Advanced; History; Social sciences; Foreign languages; Economics; French; German

Schools
Roman Catholic; Comprehensive; Public; State; Church; Church of England

Educands
Primary; University; Secondary; Adults; Children; Females; Higher; Mentally handicapped; Dyslexia; Immigrants; Blind; Physically handicapped; Students; Polytechnics; Working class; Middle class; Male; Deaf; Partially sighted

Now turn to frame 62.

62 If we examine the list in the foregoing frame carefully, it will be apparent that in some categories further subdivision is possible. This may be of two kinds, depending upon whether or not the terms within a category are mutually exclusive.

Where the terms are not mutually exclusive there will be an overlapping of definition, so that some of the terms may be combined together in order to specify a compound subject. For example, in the **Curriculum** category *Elementary* and *Science* are not mutually exclusive; the concept of *Elementary* includes the various *subjects* (*eg science*) which may be taught at that level, and similarly the concept of *science* includes all the *levels* at which that subject may be taught. Together the concepts *science* and *elementary* form the *compound subject* of *Elementary science*. The relationship is illustrated by the following diagram.

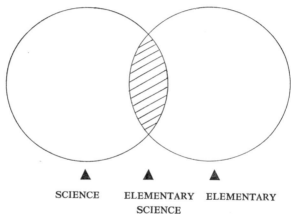

SCIENCE   ELEMENTARY   ELEMENTARY
             SCIENCE

The terms reflect different sub-characteristics within the Curriculum category, *ie* they belong to different sub-categories: Curriculum by subject (*Science*) and Curriculum by level (*Elementary*).

We can now examine each of our categories in turn, in the order in which they are listed in frame 61, to see whether or not they include sub-categories. For the present simply note in each case whether or not you believe any sub-categories may be identified, it is not necessary yet to name them. Then turn to frame 63.

63 The following categories include sub-categories:
Place; Common subdivisions; Operations; Properties; Curriculum; Schools; Educands

Now examine each of these categories, and identify the sub categories in each. The procedure will be the same as we followed in identifying the broad categories in our subject, that is to say we will examine each term and ask ourselves what characteristic it reflects within the context of the broad category within which it is included. For example, in the **Place** category *Scotland* reflects the characteristic of country or geo-political area, as also do *Ulster* and *United Kingdom*; however, *Areas of slum housing* clearly reflects a different characteristic, that of socio-economic character. As the remaining terms fall into one or other of these two sub-categories we conclude that these are the only ones to be identified in our Place category. We can now allocate terms as follows:

Place

Geo-political
Scotland; Ulster; United Kingdom; United States; England; Australia; Wales; Victoria; South Australia

Socio-economic character
Areas of slum housing; Rural; Urban

Now examine the remaining sub-categories identified above and identify the sub-categories in each, but do not yet allocate terms. Note that in some cases there may be more than two sub-categories. When you have completed this task turn to frame 64.

64 The sub-categories are as follows:
Common sub-divisions
  Common form divisions; Common subject divisions
Operations
  Administrative; Educational
Properties
  Qualifications; Terms of attendance; Marital status
Curriculum
  Subjects; Levels
Schools
  By owner; By basis of selection
Educands
  By stage of education; By age; By sex; By country of origin; By handicap; By socio-economic status
We should now allocate terms to these sub-categories. Begin with the first three of the categories listed above, allocate terms to the sub-categories in each, and then turn to frame 65.

---

65 Terms should have been allocated as follows:
Common subdivisions
  Common form divisions
    Prospectuses; Periodicals
  Common subject divisions
    Standards; Vocabulary; Research
Operations
  Administrative
    Provision; Recruitment; Purchase; Promotion
  Educational
    Teaching
Properties
  Qualifications;
    Graduate; Non-graduate
  Terms of attendance
    Part-time; Full-time
  Marital status
    Married
Now do the same for the three remaining categories, and then turn to frame 66.

66 The three remaining categories divide up as follows:
Curriculum
  Subjects
    Science; Anthropology; Chemistry; Domestic science; Sport; Reading; English language; English literature; Physical education; History; Social sciences; Foreign languages; Economics; French; German
  Levels
    Elementary; Advanced
Schools
  By owner
    Roman Catholic; Public; State; Church; Church of England
  By basis of selection
    Non-selective
Educands
  By stage of education
    Primary; University; Secondary; Higher; Polytechnic
  By age
    Adults; Children
  By sex
    Females; Males
  By country of origin
    Immigrants
  By handicap
    Mentally handicapped; Dyslexia; Blind; Physically handicapped; Deaf; Partially sighted
  By socio-economic status
    Working class; Middle class
We should now examine the various sub-categories to see if further division is possible. There is one case where this is so: Educands by handicap divides into further sub-categories of **Mentally handicapped** (*Dyslexia*) and *Physically handicapped* (*Blind*; *Deaf*; *Partially sighted*).

This completes our analysis of sub-categories, but it does not complete our subject analysis. Further grouping is possible, but of a different kind. For example it is clear that under **Educands by physical handicap** *Blind* and *Partially sighted* form a sub-group apart from *Deaf*. We shall now examine this problem.

Please turn to frame 79.

67 No, you are wrong.

It can in no sense be said that it is an essential characteristic of persons who are *graduates* that they are agents. Indeed, they may not be agents; they could be students (*ie* post-graduate students). Moreover, to assign the term *graduate* to the **Agents** category is to misunderstand the concept involved. The concept is not the person, as it is in the **Agents** category, but the qualification the person possesses. However, we should not, at this stage, assign *graduate* to a **Qualifications** category, since qualifications forms part of a wider category.

Now go back to frame 28, and attempt the question at the foot of the frame again.

---

68 The purpose of the subject analysis so far carried out is to establish the subject relationships which exist between isolate concepts within our subject; thus, for example, we have noted that *Blind* and *Deaf* each form part of a sub-category of Physically handicapped, and that *Blind* belongs to the same sequence as *Partially sighted.* The recognition of such relationships is crucial in determining the efficiency of a structured index language, for if we were conducting a search for published information on *The education of physically handicapped persons,* material on education of deaf or blind persons would clearly be relevant, and similarly material on the education of the blind, or on the education of partially sighted persons, could be relevant to a search on either subject.

We have now completed our basic subject analysis, and at this point the techniques of index language construction begin to diverge, according to the particular kind of structured index language we wish to devise. We are, at this stage, approximately 40 per cent of the way through the programme (assuming you wish to study the techniques involved in the construction of all three types of language). This is, therefore, a convenient point to break your study if you wish. If you do so you can then examine frame 84 and resume with this frame, in order to pick up the sequence.

When you have completed this frame please turn to frame 69.

69 Index languages may be divided into two broad groups, distinguished by the way in which they specify compound subjects (*ie* subjects consisting of two or more concepts in combination). The first group is known as PRE-COORDINATE, and it includes all methods of indexing in which compound subjects are entered as units under a single heading which represents all the concepts which together make up the subject, *eg* Education, Elementary (Sears *List of subject headings*), or 372 (Dewey *Decimal Classification*). In a pre-coordinate index a compound subject would normally receive only one entry, under a heading standing for that subject; a searcher looks for that heading in the index and finds entered at that point, under the heading in question, full details (author, title, etc) of the relevant documents. In other words, in a pre-coordinate index, the elements of a compound subject are put together (coordinated), by the indexer, in advance of (pre-) the search.

The second group of structured index languages is known as POST-COORDINATE, and we shall look at this group later.

What are the essential features of a pre-coordinate index language?

When you have answered this question turn to frame 70.

---

70 You should have answered that pre-coordinate means that the elements of a subject are put together by the indexer, before a search, to form a single heading under which documents on that subject are entered in the index. If your answer did not cover these points you should re-read frame 76.

If you wish to follow the programme in its entirety, to gain an insight into the principles of each of the kinds of index language studied, turn now to frame 71.

If you wish to study only pre-coordinate languages, turn now to frame 71.

If you wish to study only *either* classification schemes *or* alphabetical lists of subject headings, turn now to frame 71.

If you wish to study only post-coordinate index languages turn now to frame 172.

71 Because a pre-coordinate index includes multi-concept headings, the index language has to provide rules to govern the order in which the diverse concepts are cited within such headings, *ie* an order in which the various concepts, or terms representing them, are to be combined. Since these various terms will necessarily be taken from different categories or sub-categories (for within a category, or sub-category, the terms are mutually exclusive, and therefore incapable of combination) the formulation of these rules requires the establishment of an order of precedence, or significance, amongst the various categories and sub-categories. This is variously known as a *citation order*, or *significance order*, or *combination order*. We will use the term *combination order* as being the one which most accurately describes the process. It is important because it determines the aspect of a subject around which material will be collected, *ie* it determines the pattern of collocation in the index. For example, if we decide that *Curriculum* should be cited first, then all entries for *Science* in Education will be together, because *Science* will be a term in the primary category, whereas terms from other categories will be subordinated, and therefore entries for those subjects scattered, *eg Science* in the *primary* school, Sport in the *primary* school, Reading in the *primary* school, would be entered under *Science*, *Sport*, and *Reading* respectively.

What do you understand by combination order, and why is it important?

When you have answered this question turn to frame 72.

72 You should have answered to the effect that combination order is the order in which terms from the various categories and sub-categories are combined for the purpose of specifying compound subjects (*ie* expressly identifying compound subjects) in a pre-coordinate index. It is important because it determines the pattern of collocation in any index based on our index language.

If you answered to this effect turn now to frame 73; if not, read on.

In a pre-coordinate system compound subjects are entered under single headings which represent a combination of the terms which together identify the subject. To ensure consistency we need to have rules which determine the order in which the individual terms are to be cited. This involves establishing an order of precedence, or significance, amongst the various categories and sub-categories, for since the terms within the individual categories and sub-categories are mutually exclusive, it follows that the terms which together identify a compound subject must come from different categories and/or sub-categories. For example, item 4 in the list in frame 5 (*Roman Catholic schools in Ulster*) comprises terms from two categories: **Place** (*Ulster*) and **Schools** (*Roman Catholic*). We require a rule which will tell us, in constructing a heading for this subject, whether we should put the term from the **Place** category first (Ulster—Roman Catholic schools), or the term from the **Schools** category (Roman Catholic schools—Ulster). The rule will also, inevitably, determine whether all entries for material on education in Ulster schools will be collocated under Ulster, *eg* Ulster—State schools, Ulster—Comprehensive schools, Ulster—Church schools, etc, or scattered under the various kinds of school, *eg* Church schools—Ulster, and so on.

Thus combination order determines the order in which the various terms, which together describe a compound subject, are assembled in the heading for that subject. It is important because it also determines the pattern of collocation, that is it determines which aspects of a subject are scattered in the resulting index and which are kept together (collocated).

Turn to frame 73.

73 There are certain precepts which we may observe in deciding on a combination order. Certain patterns of subordination are usually recognized as being helpful, *eg parts* to *wholes, means* to *ends, agents* to *operations.* Part of the value of recognizing fundamental categories lies in the fact that we can organize them into a generalized combination order, thus E J Coates[1] has advanced *Thing—Part—Material—Action—Property* as a possible combination order, and *Place—Time—Common subdivisions* are generally recognized as being of least importance and as having that order. (We may note in passing, however, that in some subjects, for example History or Geography, Place may become a primary characteristic).

There are, in addition, certain principles which may sometimes be useful, though they should never be regarded as sacrosanct.

i) *Decreasing concreteness.* It is usually helpful to give precedence to the more concrete of two categories.

ii) *Consensus.* The pattern of collocation (*ie* the pattern of aspects brought together by our combination order) will usually be helpful if it reflects the usual approach of scholars and students.

iii) *Purpose.* It will usually be helpful if the primary category reflects the purpose for which the subject is studied.

The various principles and precepts here set out will often be found helpful in a neutral situation (*ie* where the index language is being drawn up without reference to any particular library, or any particular group of *users*), though even then the practical needs of the subject may take precedence. However, when an index language is being designed for a known library situation, the needs of the users in that library should be paramount, and the combination order, and resulting collocation, should reflect those needs which should be ascertained by consultation.

In a neutral situation, what do you consider should be the primary category in Education?

Curriculum—turn to frame 77.

Educands—turn to frame 85.

Schools—turn to frame 76.

1 Coates, E J: *Subject catalogues: headings and structure,* Library Association, 1960, Chapter 6.

74 Good.

We are making good progress, but we have not yet identified all the broad categories. We will therefore continue.

What characteristic is reflected by *provision* in item 7?

Problems—turn to frame 11.

Operations—turn to frame 28.

---

75 No, you are wrong again.

You have still not grasped the point that we are concerned with identifying the broad categories to which a term belongs. Having established, quite correctly, that film-strips are a form of audio-visual aid, you should have proceeded further and asked yourself whether there is any broader (more general) category to which all audio-visual aids belong. There are, in fact, two broader categories. Audio-visual aids are all teaching aids, and can therefore be placed in a broader **Teaching aids** category; but then all teaching aids (and therefore all audio-visual aids with them) can be assigned to a broader **Equipment** category. It is important that these broader relationships be recognized, otherwise we may obscure the relationship of film-strips to, say, other teaching aids.

To make quite sure that you have grasped this point re-read frame 19.

---

76 No.

As between **Educands** and **Schools**, which latter category is concerned not with the fabric but with abstract concepts such as ownership, **Educands** is the more concrete. Similarly, **Educands** is more concrete than **Curriculum.** More importantly, the principle of purpose seems to favour **Educands** as the most significant category, for the purpose of studying Education is to educate people more effectively.

We will, therefore, adopt **Educands** as our primary category.

Turn now to frame 85.

77 No.

The **Curriculum** category is certainly important, and will have quite a high priority in our combination order. However, the principle of purpose seems to indicate that **Educands** should be our primary category, since the purpose of studying Education is to educate people more effectively; moreover, as between **Educands** and **Curriculum,** or **Educands** and **Schools,** the former would seem to be the more concrete (**Schools** being concerned not with the fabric but with abstract concepts related to the organization of institutions).

We will, therefore, adopt **Educands** as our primary category.

Turn now to frame 85.

---

78 No, you have made the same mistake again.

This category is too narrow. Although *comprehensive schools* does specify schools by basis of selection (*ie* no selection), to recognize this as the broad category is to obscure the relationship with schools specified by some other characteristic, such as ownership. *Comprehensive schools*, therefore, belongs to a wider category than that of **Basis of selection**, and *state schools* belong to a wider category than that of **Ownership**; they both belong to a category of schools, or **Schools** (the latter term is preferred as being more comprehensive).

Turn now to frame 25.

79 A different kind of sub-arrangement within a category occurs when *mutually exclusive terms* may be arranged according to different characteristics. For example, within **Curriculum by subject** we can group together the various *Sciences*, *Humanities*, and so on, and within Humanities we can group together *Foreign languages*.

The situation is illustrated by the accompanying diagram.

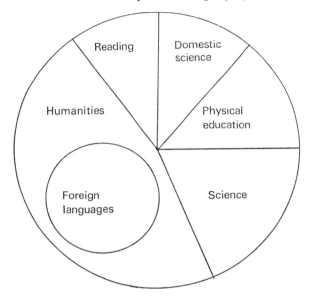

The important distinction to be made between the kind of sub-grouping illustrated above and the sub-categories previously identified, is that the terms with which we are now concerned are mutually exclusive, consequently there is no question of our being able to combine terms from different sub-groups to form compound subjects. A comparison of the above diagram with that given in frame 64 may help to make this clear.

To avoid confusion with sub-categories of the kind already identified we shall refer to this latest type of grouping as a *sequence*.

What is the important distinction to be made between a *sequence* and a sub-category?

When you have answered this question turn to frame 80.

80 You should have answered that terms from different sub-categories can be combined to form a compound subject, whereas within a category the terms in the various sequences are mutually exclusive and thus cannot be combined to form compound subjects. If your answer was not to this effect re-read frame 79 before proceeding.

We can now proceed to identify the various sequences within the categories and sub-categories already identified. Examine each category and sub-category and make a note of those in which you can identify sequences. Do not at this stage list the terms. Having done this, turn to frame 81.

---

81 The categories and sub-categories which include different sequences are as follows:

Place, Geo-political; Place, Socio-economic; Time; Equipment; Agents; Operations, Administrative; Curriculum by subject; Schools by owner; Educands by stage of education; Educands, by physical handicap.

We shall now examine each of these in turn, in each case naming the sequences and allocating to them the appropriate terms. For example:

Place

Geo-political

United Kingdom—Scotland, Ulster, England, Wales; United States; Australia—Victoria, South Australia

The reason for identifying such sequences is, again, to identify important relationships, for example that between the United Kingdom and its constituent countries, or between Australia and the various states.

Now identify the sequences in the following categories and sub-categories, and allocate the terms. Then turn to frame 82. **Place, Socio-economic; Time; Equipment; Agents; Operations.**

82 The sequences, and the terms in each, are as follows :
Place
  Socio-economic
    Urban—Areas of slum housing; Rural
Time
  19th century; 20th century—1930's, 1970's; 18th century
Equipment
  Teaching aids—Climbing frames, Books, Audio-visual aids—
  Overhead projectors, Video tapes, Television, Film-strips; Furni-
  ture—Desks, Chairs
Agents
  Educational—Teachers, Inspectors; Home environment—
  Parents
Operations
  Administrative
    Provision—Purchase; Staffing—Recruitment, Promotion
  Now do the same for the remaining categories and sub-
categories:
  **Curriculum by subject; Schools by owner; Educands by stage of
education; Educands by physical handicap.** Then turn to frame 83.

83 The analysis of the remaining categories and sub-categories into sequences is as follows:

Curriculum
Subject
Science—Anthropology, Chemistry; Domestic science; Physical education—Sport; Reading; Humanities—English—Language, Literature History Foreign languages—French, German; Social sciences—Economics

Schools
By owner
Public (*ie* Independent)—Church—Roman Catholic, Church of England; State

Educands
By stage of education
Primary; Secondary; Higher—Universities, Polytechnics
By handicap
Sight—Blind, Partially sighted; Hearing—Deaf

Now turn to frame 84.

84 The basic analysis of our subject is now completed. The full basic analysis is as follows. Note that synonyms may be identified at this stage (they are indicated below by =).

Place
Geo-political
United Kingdom—Scotland, Ulster = Northern Ireland, England, Wales; United States; Australia—Victoria, South Australia
Socio-economic
Urban—Areas of slum housing; Rural
Time
19th century; 20th century—1930's 1970's; 18th century
Common subdivisions
Common form divisions
Prospectuses; Periodicals
Common subject divisions
Standards; Vocabulary; Research
Equipment
Teaching aids—Climbing frames, Books, Audio-visual aids—Overhead projectors, Video tapes, Television, Film-strips; Furniture—Desks, Chairs
Agents
Educational—Teachers, Inspectors; Home environment—Parents
Operations
Administrative
Provision—Purchase; Staffing—Recruitment, Promotion
Educational
Teaching
Properties
Qualifications
Graduate; Non-graduate
Terms of attendance
Part-time; Full-time
Marital status
Married

84 (*cont*)
Facilities
  Libraries; Playgrounds; Laboratories; Classrooms
Teaching methods
  Programmed learning; Popularisation
Curriculum
  Subjects
    Science—Anthropology, Chemistry; Domestic science; Physical education—Sport; Reading; Humanities—English—Language, Literature, History; Foreign languages—French, German; Social sciences—Economics
  Levels
    Elementary; Advanced
Schools
  By owner
    Public (= Independent = Private)—Church—Roman Catholic (= Catholic), Church of England (= Anglican); State (= Government)
  By basis of selection
    Comprehensive (= Non-selective)
Educands (= Students = Pupils)
  By stage of education
    Primary; Secondary; Higher (= Tertiary)—Universities, Polytechnics
  By age
    Adults; Children
  By sex
    Females; Males
  By country of origin
    Immigrants
  By handicap
    Mentally handicapped
      Dyslexia
    Physically handicapped
      Sight—Blind, Partially sighted; Hearing—Deaf
  By socio-economic status
    Working class; Middle class
Now turn to frame 68.

85 Good, you are right.

The principle of purpose, in particular, points to **Educands** as the most important category.

Schools is probably not a very important category, and would not be highly favoured by any of the three principles of *decreasing concreteness, purpose,* or *consensus*; it is concerned with abstract concepts such as ownership, we do not study Education in order to provide any particular kind of school, nor is the subject usually approached in this way. On the other hand **Curriculum** is an important category, and one may argue that a part of the purpose of Education is to impart subject knowledge effectively, and that the subject is sometimes approached in terms of teaching, say, Science, more effectively. So Curriculum will probably be the second category in our combination order.

We already know that Place—Time—Common subdivisions will be the last three categories, and in this order. We can probably agree, too, that Schools will have a relatively low priority, though we cannot yet place it precisely.

Our combination order as it stands may therefore be summarized thus:

Educands
Curriculum
. . . . . .
Schools
. . . . . .
Place
Time
Common subdivisions

We have yet to consider: **Equipment; Operations; Agents; Properties; Teaching methods; Facilities.**

What should be the order of **Agents, Operations,** and **Properties**?

Turn to frame 86 after answering this question.

86 The best order is probably **Operations—Agents—Properties**.

Agents would precede **Properties** on the basis of decreasing concreteness, and if we follow the order suggested by Coates then **Operations** will also precede **Properties**.[1] **Properties** would thus be the last of the three categories in question. Since we have noted already that a generally recognized pattern of subordination is that of **Agents** to **Operations**, the order becomes: **Operations—Agents —Properties**.

We should notice that what we have decided is an order only as between these three categories: we have not yet placed them in relation to **Schools**, and we may yet decide to interpolate one or more of the remaining categories.

Our next step should probably be to place **Teaching methods** and **Equipment** in relation to these three categories. The former is obviously very closely related to **Operations**, and should logically be close to it in the combination order.

Would you place **Teaching methods** immediately before, or immediately after, **Operations**.

Turn to frame 87 after answering this question.

---

1 Coates, E J: *Subject catalogues: headings and structure,* Library Association, 1960, Chapter 6.

---

87 Teaching methods would be best placed immediately following **Operations.**

Teaching methods depends upon one of the terms within the Operations category (*ie Teaching*). We would not, therefore, normally cite any teaching method without first citing *Teaching*. Hence it seems reasonable that **Teaching methods** should follow the category to which *Teaching* belongs.

Equipment is similarly closely related to **Agents**, since usually it will be used by an Agent in carrying out an Operation. It seems reasonable, therefore that **Agents** and **Equipment** should be collocated (placed together) in the combination order. But, of the two, which should take precedence?

Consider whether or not you would agree with a proposal to place **Equipment** immediately before **Agents**. Then turn to frame 88.

88 Equipment would probably be best placed immediately before **Agents.**

It seems probable that, where an agent and a term from the Equipment category are cited together, the focus of interest will lie in the equipment rather than in the agent, for example the interest in *a study of the use of television by teachers* would, in Education, lie in the study of television as a teaching aid rather than in the study of teachers.

We now, therefore, have a consolidated order of five categories:

Operations
Teaching methods
Equipment
Agents
Properties

But we have yet to place **Schools** in relation to these five, nor have we yet decided on the significance of **Facilities**.

Where would you place **Facilities** in relation to **Schools**?

When you have answered this question turn to frame 89.

89 **Facilities** is probably best placed before **Schools.**

The principle of decreasing concreteness seems to point this way, since **Facilities** is probably more concrete than the abstract concepts which are included in our **Schools** category. But in part the decision is reached in an *ad hoc* sort of way. If we consider a title such as *The provision of libraries in state schools*, even in Education (as opposed to Librarianship) the focus of interest would surely lie in the libraries and their role in the school rather than in the kind of school.

There remains the question of placing these two categories in relation to the others. We have already noted that **Schools** will have a low priority, and it is a less concrete category than any before **Properties**. Since **Properties** relates to some of the earlier categories but not to **Schools**, it seems unnecessary to place the latter ahead of **Properties**, so we will place it immediately before Place.

Facilities are used by teachers and students, and so are analogous to equipment; it is suggested therefore that this category might be placed immediately before, or immediately after, **Equipment**. In item 7 in frame 5 (*Standards for the provision of books in school libraries*) the focus of interest probably lies in the libraries rather than in the books, and in a sense the facility within which a piece of equipment is used provides, so to speak, the context. It is suggested, therefore, that **Facilities** be placed immediately before **Equipment**.

We now have a complete citation order for our broad categories, which is set out in full in frame 90.

90 The full citation order for our broad categories is:

Educands
Curriculum
Operations
Teaching methods
Facilities
Equipment
Agents
Properties
Schools
Place
Time
Common subdivisions

Please turn now to frame 91.

91 Just as we need a combination order for our broad categories, so also we shall need a combination order for the sub-categories which we have identified within certain categories, since terms from these sub-categories are capable of being combined. There are no standard formulas for organizing sub-categories; one can only experiment to establish on a pragmatic basis what seems to be the most important sub-category, *ie* the sub-category around which material assigned to the broad category should be collected. Thus in the **Educands** category, if we make **Stage of Education** the primary sub-category, then all aspects of, for example, *Primary* education will be collocated within the **Educands** category, but aspects of education of *handicapped* persons will be scattered, since the education of handicapped persons at a particular level will be placed with the level, *eg The education of physically handicapped children at primary level* would be placed under *primary* education.

The **Educands** category is worked out below as an example.

In our **Educands** category we have the following sub-categories: **By stage of education; By age; By sex; By country of origin; By handicap; By socio-economic status**.

It seems reasonably clear that the two most important sub-categories are **By stage of education** and **By handicap**. One can envisage library situations where either of these might be the major sub-category, but in a neutral situation a document on, say, *Secondary education of physically handicapped children* would probably be most usefully collocated with material on secondary education. So **By stage of education** will be our major sub-category. A document on *The education of physically handicapped children* (**By age** and **By handicap**) would probably be regarded as having as its main focus of interest the education of the handicapped, whilst one on *The education of migrant children* would probably have the education of immigrants as its focus. If we experiment in this way, by trying out various combinations, we will probably arrive at the following combination order:

Educands
    By stage of education
    By handicap
    By country of origin

91 (*cont*)
By socio-economic status
By age
By sex
We shall also need a combination order for **Physically handicapped** and **Mentally handicapped**. There seems no very clear advantage except that, educationally, a mental handicap is likely to be a greater disadvantage, and therefore likely to pose more serious educational problems, than a physical handicap. Accordingly we will cite **Mentally handicapped** first.

The full combination order for our **Educands** category is, therefore:

Educands
    By stage of education
    By handicap
      Mentally handicapped
      Physically handicapped
    By country of origin
    By socio-economic status
    By age
    By sex

Turn now to frame 92.

---

92 You will recall that the other categories which include sub-categories are:
Curriculum
    Subjects; Levels
Operations
    Educational; Administrative
Properties
    Qualifications; Marital status; Terms of attendance
Schools
    By owner; By basis of selection
Place
    Geo-political; By socio-economic character
Common sub-divisions
    Common form divisions; Common subject divisions
Now decide a combination order for the sub-categories in the **Curriculum** category, then turn to frame 93.

93 Subjects should probably be the primary category.

This seems a fairly straightforward decision. We will surely prefer to group together our material by subject (everything about *Science* together, and everything about *History*), rather than group by level at the cost of scattering material on each subject according to the level of treatment discussed. The combination order will, therefore, be:

Curriculum
    Subjects
    Levels

Now establish a combination order for the sub-categories in the **Operations** category, and then turn to frame 94.

---

94 Educational operations will be the primary category.

In an index language for Education this decision seems quite straightforward. The combination order will thus be:

Operations
    Educational
    Administrative

Now establish a combination order for the **Properties** category, then turn to frame 95.

95 *Qualifications—Terms of service—Marital status*

With three sub-categories to arrange the problem is a little more complex than the ones you have handled in the immediately foregoing frames. Nevertheless, we should proceed in the same pragmatic way. If we had documents on *The employment of graduate married* women as teachers, or on *The part-time employment of graduates,* in either case we would probably regard graduate as being the more significant term (compared with *married* or *part-time* respectively). Similarly, if we had a document on *The part-time employment of married women,* it is probably more significant that the document is about part-time employment than that it is about the employment of married women. We may, therefore, regard **Qualifications** as the primary sub-category, and **Marital status** as the least significant. The combination order is thus:

Properties
　Qualifications
　Terms of attendance
　Marital status

Now establish a combination order for the **Schools** category, and then turn to frame 96.

3

96 The primary category should probably be **By basis of selection.**

From an educational point of view the question of whether or not a school is selective is probably more important than the question of its ownership, *ie* in a document on *Roman Catholic comprehensive schools* the primary interest would probably lie in their being comprehensive rather than in their ownership by the Roman Catholic Church. Hence the suggested combination order is:

Schools
    By basis of selection
    By ownership

Now establish a combination order for the sub-categories in the **Place** category, then turn to frame 97.

---

97 The primary sub-category within the **Place** category will be **Geo-political** place.

If we imagine documents on *Rural schools in Scotland, Rural schools in Victoria,* and *Urban schools in Scotland,* it seems clear that we would wish to keep together aspects of schools in Scotland rather than aspects of rural schools. The various schools in Scotland have more in common with one another, as being parts of a common educational system, than have rural schools in Scotland with rural schools in other areas. So the combination order should be:

Place
    Geo-political
    Socio-economic characteristics

Now establish a combination order for the sub-categories in the **Common sub-divisions** category, then turn to frame 98.

98 Common subject divisions will be the primary sub-category.
A structured index language is based upon subject analysis, and the establishment of a combination order is an integral part of the subject analysis which goes to make a pre-coordinate index language. Given a choice, in that analysis, between two sub-categories, only one of which implies any subject limitation, then the one which does imply subject limitation should take precedence. We noted earlier, when we identified the **Common sub-divisions** category, that **Common subject divisions** imposed a subject limitation, whereas **Common form divisions** did not. Accordingly the former should be the primary sub-category, and the combination order suggested is:

Common sub-divisions
Common subject divisions
Common form divisions

We now have a complete combination order for our subject, and it is set out in full in frame 99.

99 The completed combination order is:
Educands
    By stage of education
    By handicap
    By country of origin
    By socio-economic status
    By age
    By sex
Curriculum
    By subjects
    By levels
Operations
    Educational
    Administrative
Teaching methods
Facilities
Equipment
Agents
Properties
    Qualifications
    Terms of attendance
    Marital status
Schools
    By basis of selection
    By owner
Place
    Geo-political
    By socio-economic character
Time
Common sub-divisions
    Common subject divisions
    Common form divisions
Turn now to frame 100.

100 Having established a combination order for our subject, we can use the subject analysis as the basis of either of the two kinds of pre-coordinate structured index language:

i) a classification scheme

ii) an alphabetical list of subject headings.

From this point the procedure involved diverges.

If you wish to study the procedure involved in each kind of pre-coordinate structured index language—turn to frame 101.

If you wish to study only the procedure involved in making a classification scheme—turn to frame 101.

If you wish to study only the procedure involved in making an alphabetical list of subject headings—turn to frame 126.

101 The work we have carried out so far will help to form the basis of the *schedules* of our classification scheme. The schedules consist of the terms of our subject, arranged in a systematic order, together with a notation which constitutes the vocabulary of the index language since it stands for the terms in the schedules and is the medium by which entries in an index will be arranged.

We must be clear that the most important factor in a classification scheme is its *order*, that is to say the order of the schedules. This order is decided by our subject analysis, both that which we have completed, and that which we have yet to consider: it is emphatically *not* decided by the notation. The notation is subsidiary to the order, it is an auxiliary; notation should reflect order, not determine it. We must now consider this question of schedule order, and in doing so we shall begin with the basic analysis which we have carried out so far.

What will be the next step in compiling a classification scheme?

Decide on the order of terms—turn to frame 106.
Decide on the notation—turn to frame 109.

102 Good.

The subject of *Australian education* is more general than the subject of *Science in Australian education,* and more general than the subject of *Primary education in Australia,* whilst all three are more general than the subject of *Science in Australian primary education.* The relationship may be represented diagrammatically:

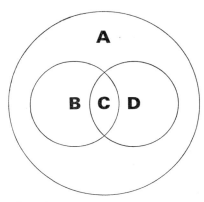

A = Australian education
B = Science in Australian education
C = Science in Australian primary education
D = Primary education in Australia

Your order preserves an order of general before special, and it also collocates subjects including terms from the primary category (**Educands**). But, the order of categories is the reverse of the combination order, being **Place—Curriculum—Educands**, whereas the combination order is **Educands—Curriculum—Place.**

This illustrates the *Principle of Inversion,* which states that, if we wish to preserve a schedule order of general before special, then the order of categories and sub-categories in the schedules will be the reverse of the combination order

Now turn to frame 112.

103 Below are four subjects, with an indication within parentheses of the categories—stated in the correct citation order as already determined—from which the constituent terms are taken. They are given in three alternative sequences. Examine each sequence carefully, bearing in mind our two requirements; observance of general before special in the linear sequence of terms in the schedule, and thus also of entries in the index, and maintenance of the pattern of collocation required by our combination order which determines the order in which we combine the terms to specify compound subjects of individual documents. Having examined the alternative sequences carefully, decide which gives the most helpful order.

a) Modern education (Time)
British education today (Place—Time)
Reading in modern education (Curriculum—Time)
Reading in modern British education (Curriculum—Place—Time)

b) Reading in modern education (Curriculum—Time)
Reading in modern British education (Curriculum—Place—Time)
British education today (Place—Time)
Modern education (Time)

c) Reading in modern British education (Curriculum—Place—Time)
Reading in modern education (Curriculum—Time)
British education today (Place—Time)
Modern education (Time)

Sequence A—turn to frame 105.
Sequence B—turn to frame 104.
Sequence C—turn to frame 110.

104 No.

The sequence you have selected does not maintain an order of general before special. You have observed an order of general before special as between the two titles which include terms from the Curriculum category, but the overall order still places the most general subject—*Modern education*—last.

When we speak of subjects being 'more general' or 'more special' than others, we mean something quite precise; thus *Modern British education* is more special than *Modern education* because the former is wholly included within the latter, it is a part of it. If you like to imagine a cake labelled 'Modern education' we could cut a slice from that cake which could be the 'British' element. In the diagram below the segment labelled 'British' represents *Modern British education*:

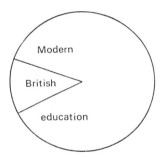

In our list of four subjects *Modern British education* and *Reading in modern education* are each part of *Modern education,* the latter must therefore be placed ahead of them as it is more general. *Reading in modern British education* is a part of the subject of *Modern British education,* and a part also of the subject of *Reading in modern education*; it must therefore be placed after them. So *Modern education* must come first in the sequence, and *Reading in modern British education* must come last. In terms of 'general before special' there is no relationship between *Modern British education* and *Reading in modern education,* for neither one is wholly included within the other (*ie* neither forms part of the other). But according to our combination order, we should collocate the

3*

104 (*cont*)

two subjects which include terms from the **Curriculum** category, since this is the most important of the three categories represented in our list. *Reading in modern education* should, therefore, be placed in third position, in order to be collocated with *Reading in modern British education* and to remain ahead of it in the sequence.

We thus arrive at the order:

Modern education (Time)

Modern British education (Place—Time)

Reading in modern education (Curriculum—Time)

Reading in modern British education (Curriculum—Place—Time)

Study this frame carefully, then go back to frame 107.

---

105 Good.

Notice that the order you have selected means that the categories appear in the *reverse* of the order in which they are cited in specifying a compound subject. Schedule order for the three categories in our list is Time—Place—Curriculum, but the combination order is Curriculum—Place—Time. If we wish to maintain an order of general before special in the schedules of a classification scheme, the order of categories in the schedules will be the reverse of the order of categories in the combination order. This is known as the *Principle of Inversion*.

Now turn to frame 112.

106 Good.

The order in which the terms were listed within the various categories and sub-categories in our basic analysis is purely a random order, and the only order we have established so far is a combination order. This combination order is an order for combining terms in specifying a compound subject, and it is not necessarily the same as the *schedule* order; *ie* the order in which we combine terms from various categories and sub-categories, when we have to specify a compound subject, is not necessarily the same as the order in which they are set out in the schedules. Schedule order is the order in which terms are listed in the schedules, and is thus related to the order of *various* documents on the shelves, or of entries in an index for *various* documents; combination order is the order in which terms are combined to specify the compound subject of *one* document.

What we require in the schedules is an order which will be helpful to users. Now, it is usually considered that a helpful sequence will place general subjects ahead of more special subjects, *ie* the sequence should proceed from general to special. So, for example, in Literature *Verse* and *English* should precede *English verse,* since the first two subjects are more general than *English verse;* the subject of *English verse* is part of, and wholly included within, the wider subjects of *English* literature and also *Verse.* The accompanying diagram illustrates the relationships.

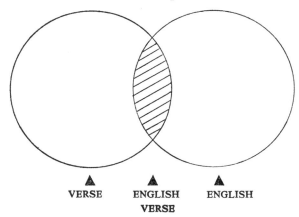

▲   ▲   ▲
VERSE   ENGLISH   ENGLISH
VERSE

Study this diagram, and when you think you have grasped the point turn to frame 107.

107 The order in which the terms are listed must also permit us to keep together subjects which include terms from our primary category. In Literature we would certainly cite *Language* before *Literary form*, so *English literature* and *English verse* should be kept together. The order of our three subjects must, therefore, be: *Verse*; *English literature*; *English verse*—no other order will meet both our requirements: general before special, and collocation of aspects of *English* literature.

Below are four subjects, with an indication within parentheses of the categories—stated in the combination order previously determined—from which the constituent terms are taken. They are given in three alternative sequences. Examine each sequence carefully, bearing in mind both requirements as just noted, and decide which sequence gives the most helpful order.

a) Australian education (Place)
   Science in Australian education (Curriculum—Place)
   Primary education in Australia (Educand—Place)
   Science in Australian primary education (Educand—Curriculum
   —Place)

b) Primary education in Australia (Educand—Place)
   Science in Australian primary education (Educand—Curriculum
   —Place)
   Science in Australian education (Curriculum—Place)
   Australian education (Place)

c) Science in Australian primary education (Educand—Curriculum
   —Place)
   Primary education in Australia (Educand—Place)
   Science in Australian education (Curriculum—Place)
   Australian education (Place)

Sequence A—turn to frame 102.
Sequence B—turn to frame 111.
Sequence C—turn to frame 108.

The subject of *Australian education* is more general than the subject of *Science in Australian education,* and more general than the subject of *Primary education in Australia*; all three are more general than the subject of *Science in Australian primary education.* The relationships may be represented diagrammatically:

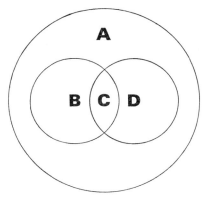

A = Australian education
B = Science in Australian education
C = Science in Australian primary education
D = Primary education in Australia

The order which you have selected is the same as the combination order, but you will recall that combination order is concerned with the order in which terms from different categories and/or sub-categories are combined in specifying compound subjects; it is not concerned with schedule order, which is the sequence in which terms are listed in the scheme. We have noted that it is generally accepted that a helpful order will observe a sequence of general before special. Now, the most general subject in the list was *Australian education,* but the order you have selected places this last; the most special subject was *Science in Australian primary education,* but the order you have selected places this first.

Try another example. Turn to frame 103 and look at the titles listed there.

109 No.

You have evidently not grasped the important fact that the notation ought to be strictly subordinate to the order of the schedules. The basic function of notation is to maintain and mechanize the order of terms in the schedules, and it can only do this effectively, and without disrupting that order, if the order is determined first.

Our next step, therefore, will be to determine the order of the schedules.

Now turn to frame 103.

Your chosen sequence still does not maintain an order or general before special. In fact your order is precisely the reverse: it proceeds from special to general.

When we speak of subjects being 'more general' or 'more special' than others we mean something quite precise; thus *Modern British education* is more special than *Modern education* because the former is wholly included within the latter, it is a part of it. If you like to imagine a cake labelled 'Modern education' we could cut a slice from that cake which could be the 'British' element. In the diagram below the portion labelled 'British' represents *Modern British Education*:

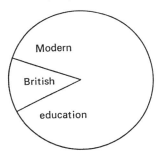

In our list of four subjects *Modern British education* and *Reading in modern education* are each part of *Modern education*; the latter must therefore be placed before them as it is more general. *Reading in modern British education* is a part of the subject of *Modern British education*, and a part also of the subject of *Reading in modern education*; it must therefore be placed after them. So *Modern education* must come first in the sequence, and *Reading in modern British education* must come last. In terms of 'general before special' there is no relationship between *Modern British education* and *Reading in modern education*, neither one is wholly included within the other (*ie* neither forms part of the other). But according to our citation order we should collocate the two subjects which include terms from the Curriculum category, because this is the most important of the three categories represented in our list. *Reading in modern education* should, therefore,

110 (*cont*)

be placed in third position, in order to be collocated with *Reading in modern British education.*

We thus arrive at the order:

Modern education (Time)

Modern British education (Place—Time)

Reading in modern education (Curriculum—Time)

Reading in modern British education (Curriculum—Place—Time)

Study this frame carefully, then go back to frame 107.

The subject of *Australian education* is more general than the subject of Science in *Australian education*, and more general than the subject of *Primary education in Australia*; all three are more general than the subject of *Science in Australian primary education*. The relationships may be represented diagrammatically:

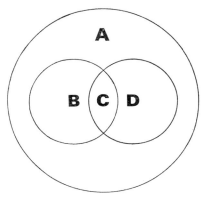

A = Australian education
B = Science in Australian education
C = Science in Australian primary education
D = Primary education in Australia

The order which you have selected is almost the reverse of what would usually be regarded as a helpful order. You may recall that we have to satisfy two conditions: we should maintain an order of general before special, and we should observe the pattern of collocation required by our combination order. You have satisfied the latter condition; our primary category is **Educands**, and you have correctly kept together the two titles which include a term from that category. You have even, within that category, placed the more general title first. But in placing the other two titles in relation to the two from the **Educands** category you have contrived to place the most general of the four titles first.

Remember the two conditions mentioned above, and try another example. Turn to frame 103 and look at the titles listed there.

112 The schedule order for categories and sub-categories is thus the reverse of the combination order—least significant first, and within a category the least significant sub-category first.

Common sub-divisions
  Common form divisions
  Common subject divisions
Time
Place
  By socio-economic character
  Geo-political
Institutions
  By owner
  By basis of selection
Properties
  Marital status
  Terms of service
  Qualifications
Agents
Equipment
Facilities
Teaching methods
Operations
  Administrative
  Educational
Curriculum
  By levels
  By subjects
Educands
  By sex
  By age
  By socio-economic status
  By country of origin
  By handicap
  By stage of education

Now turn to frame 113.

113 We must now decide the order of the terms within each category, sub-category and sequence, and also the order of the various sequences within a category. There are a number of principles which we might consider as a basis of arrangement.

One principle is that of *geographical order*, and this will clearly be the principle which we should apply in *Geo-political Place*. It means simply that the sequence should reflect what Ranganathan has called ' spatial contiguity '—*ie* neighbouring geo-political areas should be close to each other in the sequence. The country which occurs first in the sequence should be the ' home ' country of the library, or of the compiler of the index language in a neutral situation (on the assumption that the heaviest use of the system would be amongst fellow countrymen). We can, if we wish, leave a space at the beginning of the sequence for a library to insert the name of the ' home ', or ' mother ', country.

What is geographical order?

Turn to frame 114.

---

114 Geographical order is the principle by which geo-political areas are arranged according to spatial contiguity.

In some ways allied to this principle is that of *chronological order*. This applies most obviously in the **Time** category, but it can be used for some others. In our scheme we can use it for the **Operations** category, in which case the operations will be arranged according to the order in which they are carried out, for example, *Recruitment* before *Promotion*. Religions, and also Churches, can be arranged chronologically (oldest first), so *Roman Catholic Church* should be placed ahead of *Church of England*; similarly *Church schools* will precede *State schools*.

To which categories can we apply the principle of chronological order?

Turn to frame 115.

115 *Chronological order* may be used as the basis of arrangement for the categories of **Time**, of **Operations** and of **Institutions by owner**.

Evolutionary order is similar to chronological order. It is the principle that, where two or more terms stand for a line of evolution through which a person or thing passes, the term(s) representing the earlier phase(s) should precede the term(s) representing the later phase(s).

In Education a person passes through a line of evolution represented by the various stages—*Primary, Secondary, Tertiary (ie Higher)*. These may therefore be arranged in that order.

What do you understand by the *Principle of Evolutionary Order*? Where may we apply it in our scheme?

Turn to frame 116.

---

116 The *Principle of Evolutionary Order* is the principle whereby the terms representing the stages of an evolutionary process through which a person or thing passes, should be arranged with the term(s) representing the earlier phase(s) first. In our scheme we may apply it to **Educands by stage of education** and to **Educands by age**.

Less important, because less frequently applicable, is an order of *Increasing complexity*. Where a number of terms represent objects or concepts of varying degrees of complexity, the term(s) reflecting the lesser degree of complexity should precede the term(s) reflecting the greater degree of complexity. For example, plane geometry (two dimensions) should precede solid geometry (three dimensions).

What is meant by an order of *increasing complexity*?

117 An order of increasing complexity means that of a number of terms representing concepts of varying degrees of complexity, those reflecting the lesser degree of complexity should be placed first.

It sometimes happens that there is no helpful order inherent in the terms, or in their context. Where this happens we may usefully follow an order established elsewhere. For example, in a scientific classification plants and animals could usefully be arranged in a sequence established in a taxonomic classification. This is known as *canonical order*. In our scheme there is no clear sequence in which we can arrange the terms in our **Curriculum by subjects**; we may, however, usefully follow an order established elsewhere, and there is a fairly obvious source to which a librarian would turn for a list of subjects in a systematic order. We will see in a moment what this source is.

Meanwhile, what do you understand by *canonical order*?

Turn to frame 118.

---

118 *Canonical order* means that where there is no helpful order inherent in a set of terms, or in their context, it may be useful to follow an order established elsewhere.

For **Curriculum** by subject we need a list of subjects in a systematic order which we may adapt as the basis of our arrangement. We will find such a list in a general classification scheme. By common consent the order of subjects (*ie* main classes) in Bliss's Bibliographic classification is superior to that of any other general scheme, and we will base our order on that used in this scheme.

Two other principles remain :

Consistent order: where a number of terms appear at more than one point in a scheme, it may be useful if they follow a consistent order. (This mainly applies in a general classification scheme).

Alphabetical order may be adopted where no other principle applies.

Now turn to frame 119.

119 We are now almost ready to write out our terms in schedule order. In doing so we must ensure that the layout is as clear as possible, using capitalization, indentation and typography to show subordination and coordination. All synonyms should be included in the schedules, and should be indicated thus:

Northern Ireland = Ulster

The preferred term (*ie* the term adopted as the index language term) should be placed first.

The terms for our scheme are set out in schedule order in frame 120. Study this and then turn to frame 121.

Common sub-divisions
Common form divisions
  Periodicals
  Prospectuses
Common subject divisions
  Research
  Standards
  Vocabulary
Time
18th century
19th century
20th century
  1930's
  1970's
Place
By socio-economic characteristics
  Rural
  Urban
    Areas of slum housing
Geo-political
  ' Mother country '
  United Kingdom
    England
    Wales
    Scotland
    Northern Ireland = Ulster
  Australia
    Victoria
    South Australia
  United States

Schools
By owner
  Public = Independent
    Churches
      Roman Catholic

Properties
Marital status
  Married
Terms of service
  Part-time
  Full-time
Qualifications
  Non-graduate
  Graduate

Agents
Educational
  Teachers
  Inspectors
Home environment
  Parents

Equipment
Teaching aids = Edu-
  cational
  Audio-visual aids
    Overhead projectors
    Film-strips
    Television
    Video tapes
  Books
  Climbing frames
Furniture
  Chairs
  Desks

Facilities
Playgrounds
Classrooms
Laboratories
Libraries

Schools (*cont*)
  Church of England = Anglican
  State = Government
By basis of selection
  Comprehensive = Non-selective
Operations
Administration
  Provision
    Purchase
  Staffing
    Recruitment
    Promotion
  Educational
    Teaching

Curriculum
Levels
  Elementary
  Advanced
Subjects
  Reading
  Science
    Chemistry
    Anthropology
  Social sciences
    Economics
  Humanities
    History
    English
      Language
      Literature
    Foreign languages
    German
    French
  Domestic science
  Physical education
    Sport

Teaching methods
  Popularisation
  Programmed learning

Educands
By sex
  Females
  Males
By age
  Children
  Adults
By socio-economic status
  Working class
  Middle class
By country of origin
  Immigrants
By handicap
  Physical
    Sight
      Partially sighted
      Blind
    Hearing
      Deaf
  Mental
    Dyslexia
By stage of education
  Primary = Elementary
  Secondary
  Higher = Tertiary=
    Further
    Polytechnics
    Universities

121 Having now completed the listing of terms in schedule order we can add the notation.

It is the notation which will provide the vocabulary of our index language, since the 'terms' which will be used as headings in any index arranged by our classification scheme will be notational symbols. Because classification schemes use an artificial vocabulary they are sometimes referred to as *coded* index languages, as opposed to *verbal* index languages such as lists of subject headings.

The notation should possess certain qualities. It should have a clear ordinal value, it should be easy to understand, and as brief as practicable. It should provide the mechanics for synthesis (*ie* number building: the joining together of pieces of notation standing for individual terms, in order to specify compound subjects). Above all it should be hospitable; *ie* it should facilitate the insertion of new subjects as they arise, at the correct position according to the pattern of the scheme. The need for synthesis means that the notation should provide indicators, so that in a compound number it is possible to identify the component parts. Lack of this facility is apt to lead to ambiguity.

Letters give a briefer notation than numbers, because the base (A-Z) is longer than of numbers (0-9). A combination of upper case letters for the initial digit of any individual piece of notation, followed by lower case, makes a convenient notation which meets the criteria set out above reasonably well. The initial capital letter makes a clear indicator without making the notation too complex.

The schedules, complete with notation, are set out in frame 122. Study that frame carefully, and then turn to frame 123.

B EDUCATION

C	**Common subdivisions**	Gs	Victoria
Cd	Common form divisions	Gu	South Australia
Cj	Periodicals	Gx	United States
Cp	Prospectuses	H	Schools
D	Common subject divisions	Hc	By owner
Dg	Research	He	Public = Independent
Dq	Standards	Hg	Churches
Dv	Vocabulary	Hk	Roman Catholic
		Hp	Church of England = Anglican
E	**Time**		
Ek	18th century		
En	19th century	Hs	State = Government
Eq	20th century	J	By basis of selection
Eu	1930's	Jg	Comprehensive = Non-selective
Ey	1970's		
F	**Place**	K	**Properties**
Fc	Socio-economic characteristics	Kb	Marital status
		Kd	Married
Fe	Rural	Kg	Terms of attendance
Fm	Urban	Kj	Part-time
Fr	Areas of slum housing	Kl	Full-time
		Kn	Qualifications
G	Geo-political	Kq	Non-graduate
Gb	"Mother country"	Ks	Graduate
Gf	United Kingdom		
Gh	England	L	**Agents**
Gj	Wales	Le	Educational
Gl	Scotland	Lg	Teachers
Gn	Northern Ireland = Ulster	Lm	Inspectors
		Lp	Home environment
Gq	Australia	Lt	Parents

122 (*cont*)

M	Equipment	S	Subjects
Mc	Teaching aids = Educational	Sc	Reading
		Sg	Science
Me	Audio-visual aids	Sj	Chemistry
Mg	Overhead projectors	Sm	Anthropology
Mj	Film-strips	Sp	Social sciences
Mm	Television	Ss	Economics
Mp	Video tapes	T	Humanities
Mr	Books	Tf	History
Mt	Climbing frames	Tj	English
Mv	Furniture	Tk	Language
Mw	Desks	Tm	Literature
Mx	Chairs	Tp	Foreign languages
		Tr	German
N	Facilities	Tt	French
Nf	Playgrounds	Tv	Domestic science
Nj	Classrooms	Tw	Physical education
Np	Laboratories	Ty	Sport
Nt	Libraries		
		U	**Educands**
P	Teaching methods	Uc	By sex
Pj	Popularisation	Ud	Females
Pr	Programmed learning	Ue	Males
		V	By age
Q	**Operations**	Vg	Children
Qb	Administration	Vr	Adults
Qd	Provision	W	By socio-economic status
Qf	Purchase	Wd	Working class
Qh	Staffing	Wg	Middle class
Qk	Recruitment	X	By country of origin
Qn	Promotion	Xj	Immigrants
Qr	Educational	Y	By handicap
Qt	Teaching	Yd	Physical
		Yf	Sight
R	**Curriculum**	Yj	Partially sighted
Rc	Levels	Ym	Blind
Re	Elementary	Yp	Hearing
Rq	Advanced		

122 (*cont*)

Yr	Deaf	Zg	Secondary
Yt	Mental	Zk	Higher = Tertiary =
Yv	Dyslexia		Further
Z	By stage of education	Zp	Polytechnics
Zd	Primary = Elementary	Zu	Universities

123 The order of the schedules is not apparent. It reflects a considerable number of quite complex decisions as to the recognition and application of characteristics of division, combination order, and so on. Nor does our notation possess any inherent 'meaning'. We therefore require a means of translating our normal spoken and written language (*ie* natural language) into the language of our scheme—its notation. The means of doing this will lie in the provision of an alphabetical index, which will list all the terms included in the schedules in a single alphabetical sequence, indicating in each case the corresponding notation. This index thus 'translates' natural language into the language of our scheme, *ie* it acts as a dictionary, and enables us to match our vocabulary with the appropriate notation from the vocabulary of the scheme.

You will find the beginning of the index to our scheme set out in frame 124. Study it, and then turn to frame 125.

124 The index, in part, will read as follows:

Administration	Qb
Adults: Educands	Vg
Advanced level	Rq
Age: Educands	V
Agents	L
Anglican Church: Schools	Hp
Anthropology	Sm
Areas of slum housing	Fr
Audio-visual aids	Me
Australia	Gq
Basis of selection	J
Blind persons: Educands	Ym
Books	Mr
Boys	VgUe
Catholic schools	Hk
Chairs	Mx
Chemistry	Sj
Children	Vg
Church of England schools	Hp
Churches: Schools	Hg
Classrooms	Nj
Climbing frames	Mt
Common form divisions	Cd
Common subdivisions	C
Common subject divisions	D
Comprehensive schools	Jg
Curriculum	R
Deaf persons: Educands	Yr
Desks	Mx
Domestic science	Tv
Dyslexia	Yv
Economics	Ss
Educands	U
Educational agents	Le
Educational equipment	Mc
Educational operations	Qr
Elementary education	Zd
Elementary level	Re
England	Gh
English expression	Tj
English language	Tk
English literature	Tm
English studies	Tj
Equipment	M
Facilities	N
Females: Educands	Ud
Film-strips	Mj
Foreign languages	Tp
Form divisions	Cd
French language	Tt
Full-time	Kl
Furniture	Mv
Further education	Zk
Geo-political place	G
German language	Tr
Girls	VgUd
Graduate qualifications	Ks
Handicapped persons: Educands	Y
Hearing: Handicaps	Yp
Higher education	Zk
History: Curriculum	Tf
Home environment	Lp
Humanities	T

125 Our scheme is now almost complete.

You, having compiled the scheme step by step, will be fully able to use the scheme, for you will be familiar with the decisions which have been made, and of which one has to be aware in order to apply the scheme, for example the combination order. A potential user of the scheme, however will not have gone through the steps involved in constructing the scheme and will need to be informed of the various rules, and will require instruction in the use of the scheme. This you should provide in an *Introduction*. The *Introduction* should provide full and detailed instructions on the use of the scheme, *eg* explain the combination order, the mechanism of synthesis etc. It should include some examples of titles classified by the scheme, for example with our scheme:

Science in the primary school ZdSg

Standards of book provision in secondary school libraries
ZgQdNtMrDq

Domestic science for girls in primary schools ZdVgUdTv

Teaching English to immigrant children in Australia XjVgTkQtGq

If you wish to take a break from your study of this programme, this is a suitable point at which to do so. The programme continues on frame 130.

126 Good, you are quite right.

You will remember that our approach vocabulary of terms which have not been adopted for use as headings in the index (or as a part of headings), but which might nevertheless be used by readers in formulating a search. It therefore follows that, although the terms will not be entered as headings in the index, a user might look in the index for these terms, and for this reason we need signposts, in the form of *see* references, to direct such users to the term which has been employed instead. So it will be necessary, under each used term in our index language, to indicate any approach terms for which the used term stands. This is done so that the indexer, when using the vocabulary term (*ie* the used term) in a heading, will not neglect to include *in the index* an entry to guide the user who refers to the unused term, to the correct vocabulary term. For example, under **Church of England** in the list of subject headings we should find the following:

Church of England

   x Anglican

This is an instruction to the indexer, which is printed in the list, reminding him that when **Church of England** is used as a heading, he should make a *see* reference from Anglican, *ie* he should insert the following reference in the index:

Anglican

   See **Church of England**

What instruction should we provide in our subject headings list to link **Higher education** and Tertiary education?

Tertiary education

   x **Higher education**—turn to frame 150.

Higher education

   x Tertiary education—turn to frame 128.

127 I'm afraid not.

Physical education is the wider of the two subjects, **Sport** being a part of it. **Sport** is lower in the hierarchy. The two diagrams illustrate the relationship.

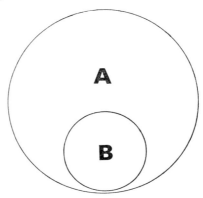

A = Physical education
B = Sport

                    Physical education
                          |
      ┌───────────────────────────────────┐
      | |
    Sport   (Other PE activities, *eg* Gymnastics)

The reference from the broader subject to the narrower, or down the hierarchy, would thus be:

Physical education
   See also **Sport**

Try another example.

Referring to the analysis in frame 84, decide how **Qualifications** and **Graduate** should be linked.

Graduate
   See also
   Qualifications—turn to frame 148.
Qualifications
   See also **Graduate**—turn to frame 145.

128 Good.

In the case of terms from the approach vocabulary, there is need for an indication of the appropriate vocabulary term as a guide to the indexer, *eg*

Disadvantaged
>   *See* **Handicapped**

This is an instruction to the indexer that Disadvantaged is not a used term, and that instead he should adopt Handicapped, to which term he should now turn. Similar instruction should be provided under each term in the approach vocabulary.

What link should we make, in our alphabetical listing, between the approach term Tertiary education and the used term **Higher education**?

Tertiary education
>   *See* **Higher education**—turn to frame 146.

Higher education
>   *See* Tertiary education—turn to frame 138.

---

129 In constructing an alphabetical list of subject headings (the second kind of pre-coordinate index language) we shall make use of our basic analysis (frame 84) and the combination order which we have established for pre-coordinate systems (frame 99). Remember that the construction of an alphabetical list of subject headings is quite independent of the construction of a classification scheme: it represents an alternative way of manipulating our basic analysis.

Turn now to frame 130.

130 Lists of subject headings in common use are largely *enumerative*, that is to say they actually list many compound headings, as well as simple terms. The alternative to an enumerative list is one which is *synthetic*, that is to say one which lists only simple terms, providing a formula (a combination order) for assembling terms from the list when a compound heading is required. In practice an enumerative list frequently fails to provide headings which specify a required subject precisely, because although the individual terms are included in the list there is no heading provided which includes all the required terms in combination. A synthetic list would be able to specify any compound subject so long as the individual terms have been included in the list. For this reason a synthetic list is likely to provide a greater degree of specification.

What do you understand by a synthetic list of subject headings, and what is the main advantage of such a list?

Turn now to frame 131.

131 A synthetic list of subject headings is one which includes only simple terms, with rules for their combination as necessary to specify compound subjects. The main advantage of such a list would be its greater range of specification as compared with an enumerative list.

For the purpose of this exercise a synthetic list is assumed. Because we already know that the sequence of terms will be alphabetical, and there is no question of using the list as a means of ordering documents or index entries in a systematic arrangement, the combination order will not be required until we add the *Introduction* to the list and provide instructions on how to use the list in indexing.

Although we have decided to construct our list on synthetic lines, there will be occasions when we shall have to use terms in combination. This is because an alphabetical listing of simple terms will sometimes fail to supply a needed context. (Notice the contrast with a classification scheme, where the systematic order and the hierarchy of the schedules, usually provides any necessary context.) For example, in an alphabetical listing *Higher* cannot stand on its own, either in the list or in a heading, we must add *education* to render it as *Higher education*. We must also decide whether to use the uninverted form, as here, or the inverted form: *Education, Higher*. We will use the uninverted form, because it corresponds with normal usage, and because it gives more direct access by providing a more specific approach.

Examine the terms in our basic analysis and make a list of terms which will need to be rendered in combination as above. Then turn to frame 132.

132 The following is a list of terms which should be rendered in combination:

Advanced level
Church of England schools
Church schools
Comprehensive schools
Elementary level
Higher education
Independent schools
Primary education
Roman Catholic schools
Secondary education
Slum housing areas
State schools

We shall also need to restore terms such as *Girls*, which represent complex (*ie* multi-aspect) concepts. *Slum housing areas* has been rendered in this inverted form in order to bring the significant term to the front.

Turn now to frame 133.

---

133 An alphabetical subject headings list usually includes within one single alphabetical sequence both the terms to be used in the index (the index vocabulary) and terms not adopted for use in the index but which might be employed by users in formulating a search (the approach vocabulary). It is usual to distinguish between the two by using **bold** type for the index vocabulary and ordinary roman type for the approach vocabulary. If we were using a typewriter we might adopt CAPITALS for the index vocabulary, in this text bold type has been used.

What is the significance of bold type in a printed list of subject headings? When you have answered please turn to frame 134.

134 You should have answered that bold type is used to indicate terms which have been adopted as the index vocabulary, *ie* it indicates used terms.

We are now almost ready to compile our alphabetical listing. Before we do so you should note a further point: that terms from the *Place, Time* and *Common sub-divisions* categories should not be included. We shall see later how these terms are handled.

Compile your own alphabetical listing of terms, and then turn to frame 135 where the list is set out. Study it, and then turn to frame 136.

135 The list is as follows:

Administration
Adults
Advanced level
Agents
Anglican schools
Anthropology
Areas of slum housing
Arts subjects
Audio-visual aids

Blind
Books
Boys

Catholic schools
Chairs
Chemistry
Children
Church of England
  schools
Church schools
Classrooms
Climbing frames
Comprehensive schools
Curriculum

Deaf
Desks
Domestic science
Dyslexia

Economics
Educands
Elementary education
Elementary level
English language
English literature
English studies
Equipment

Foreign languages

German
Girls
Government schools
Graduate

Handicapped
Hearing
Higher education
History
Home environment
Humanities

Immigrants
Independent schools
Inspectors

Laboratories
Languages
Levels
Libraries

Marital status
Married
Mentally handicapped
Middle class

Non-graduate
Non-selective

Operations
Overhead projectors

Parents
Partially sighted
Part-time
Physical education
Physically handicapped
Playgrounds
Polytechnics
Popularization

Primary education
Private schools
Programmed learning
Promotion
Properties
Public schools
Pupils
Purchase

Qualifications

Reading
Recruitment
Roman Catholic schools
Rural

Schools
Secondary education
Selection
Sight
Slum housing areas
Social sciences
Sport
Staffing
State schools
Students
Subjects

Teachers
Teaching
Teaching aids
Teaching methods
Television
Terms of attendance
Tertiary education

Universities

Video tapes

Women
Working class

136 A very important feature of an alphabetical list of subject headings is the system of *see* and *see also* references. The former are associated with vocabulary control, the latter with subject relationships (*ie* syntax). Before we examine these references it is essential to understand a basic principle: that references are always made *towards* a heading. This follows from the essential function of references, which is to act as signposts to guide a user from one part of the index to another where relevant information is likely to be found. In order to avoid making 'blind' references (references which lead to headings which have not been used, and thus to places where there is no information) references are placed in the index as a part of the procedure in constructing a heading, and are made towards the heading under construction. This ensures that references will not be blind.

If we are using **Primary education** as a heading, and an associated term is **Children,** what reference will we require?

Children
    See also **Primary education**—turn to frame 142.

Primary education
    See also **Children**—turn to frame 126.

137 No, you have made the same mistake again.

The issue, basically, is a very simple one. We have a concept which can only be rendered adequately by a combination of words, and this combination may be used in one of two constructions: uninverted—Programmed learning, or inverted—Learning, Programmed. We can adopt only one of these constructions in our index vocabulary, and we decided earlier that we would use the uninverted construction, but we cannot be certain that our users will always think of this construction; they may sometimes think of the inversion and look for it, and we must therefore provide guidance for them, to ensure that if they do think of the inverted construction, they will be guided to the alternative which we have adopted. We also need to provide guidance for the indexer, for the same reason.

Accordingly we provide guidance *in the list* for the indexer:

Learning, Programmed
> *See* **Programmed Learning**

and we provide instructions to the indexer to ensure that provision is made *in the index* for the user. This we do by instructing the indexer to provide a *see* reference *from* the unused construction *towards* the used construction, and this instruction, coded *x*, appears under the used construction:

Programmed Learning
> *x* Learning, Programmed

Consider this carefully, then turn to frame 146.

---

138 No, you are quite wrong.

The whole point is to guide the indexer, who has referred to the incorrect (*ie* unused) term, to the correct (*ie* used) term. You, however, are attempting to guide the indexer in the opposite direction, from the used term to the unused term.

What link should be made in our index language between the used term **Educands** and the unused term Students?

Educands
> *See* Students—turn to frame 149.

Students
> *See* **Educands**—turn to frame 146.

139 No.

You have not considered the point with sufficient thoroughness. Turn to frame 136 and read it carefully, thinking about the point as you go along. Remember, the fundamental principle is that one should always construct references *towards* a chosen heading.

---

140 No.

You are still confused, and still pointing your sign-post in the wrong direction. The used term, featured in bold type, is Roman Catholic, this is the point to which we wish to direct our user, and this is the term which will be used in the index. We must, therefore, provide for the indexer a reminder that he must ensure that a reader using the incorrect term is guided to the correct term. Remember, the instruction appears in the list under the *used* term; the resulting reference appears in the index under the unused term.

After reading this frame carefully turn back to frame 126.

---

141 No, you are wrong.

Since the reference is filed under **Higher education** it is clearly a direction to the user who is searching the index at that point. It is intended to direct the user to possibly related material which has been entered under the heading **Universities.**

What would be indicated by a reference:

Church schools

 See also **Roman Catholic schools**

That information related to the subject of **Church schools** may be found under the heading **Roman Catholic schools**—turn to frame 157.

That information related to the subject of **Roman Catholic schools** may also be found under the heading **Church schools**—turn to frame 143.

4*

142 No.

If we are using **Primary education,** then the only way in which we can ensure that our references are not 'blind' is by making them *towards* our chosen term. Furthermore, our concern in adopting the term **Primary education** is with the document in hand to which the term is relevant; the references we make should, therefore, be designed to direct users to this document. This is an absolutely basic principle: that references are directed towards a chosen term.

Which of the following statements is correct?

a) In selecting the term Teaching methods we should make the reference

Teaching methods
  See also **Popularization**

because a user searching for information on teaching methods might also find relevant information under the second heading.

or

b) In selecting the term Teaching methods we should make the reference

Popularization
  See also **Teaching methods**

because a user searching for information on Popularization might also find relevant information entered under the second heading.

If you selected statement (a)—turn to frame 139.
If you selected statement (b)—turn to frame 126.

---

143 No, you are still wrong.

The reference will file under **Higher education,** so clearly the information it conveys is intended for persons who are searching in the index at that point; a direction intended for persons interested primarily in **Universities** would be filed under **Universities.** A reference is always intended for the guidance of those who are searching the index under the term which is the filing medium, *ie* the heading. In our present example that term is **Higher education.**

Consider this point carefully, and then turn to frame 153 and work through it again.

144 No, you have made the same mistake again.

$$\frac{\text{\textbf{Overhead projectors}}}{xx\ \text{\textbf{Audio-visual aids}}} = \frac{\text{\textbf{Audio-visual aids}}}{\textit{See also}\ \text{\textbf{Overhead projectors}}}$$

xx means ' make a reference *away from* the term which follows ', and the reference should lead towards the heading under which the instruction appears. It is most important that you understand this point.

Consider the above example carefully, and then turn to frame 157 and work through this phase of the programme again.

145 Good, you are quite right.

In constructing these references it is very important that the terms linked should be *proximate*, *ie* that we ensure that x relationships are not concealed by omitting steps of division in the linking process. The two diagrams, and the accompanying text below, illustrate the point.

Within the Curriculum category we have several steps of division between the broadest subject—Curriculum—and the subject of French within the Humanities sub-group of the Subjects sub-category. The intermediate steps of division are indicated by the concentric rings in diagram A, or the stages of the hierarchy in diagram B. In order to display all the links between Curriculum and French we must ensure that our references proceed step by step as below.

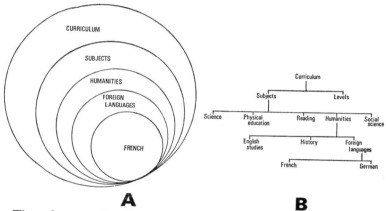

A   **B**

The references should proceed as follows:

Curriculum	**Subjects**	**Humanities**	**Foreign languages**
See also	*See also*	*See also*	*See also*
Subjects	**Humanities**	**Foreign languages**	**French**

Now examine the basic analysis in frame 84 and consider which of the following references should be made to Audio-visual aids

Equipment
   See also
Audio-visual aids—turn to frame 165.
Teaching aids
   See also
Audio-visual aids—turn to frame 163.

146 Good.

It will be recalled that we have found it necessary to use terms in combination to represent certain concepts, *eg* **Primary education, Independent schools,** and also that some of the concepts represented in our basic analysis in frame 84 have required terms in combination, *eg* **Domestic science.** We have decided to use the uninverted construction of such combinations in our headings, *eg* **Primary education,** but in many cases a reader might possibly use the inverted construction, *eg* Education, Primary. We must, therefore, treat such inverted constructions of our term combinations as synonyms. As a general rule we should do this whenever the first word of the term combination serves to qualify the second. Thus in the case of **Primary education** we would treat the inverted construction in the same way as a synonym, since Primary education is a kind of education; however, we would disregard the inverted construction of **Domestic science,** since Domestic science is not a kind of science, and it seems unlikely that a reader would use the inverted construction.

In our list of subject headings we shall need the following provision. We shall require an instruction to the indexer that in using, for example, **Primary education,** as a heading, he should provide in the index a *see* reference to guide a user turning to the incorrect construction to the correct construction:

Primary education
  x Education, Primary

We shall also need a *see* instruction in the list itself, in case the indexer turns to the incorrect construction, *ie* :

Education, Primary
  See **Primary education**

How should we treat Independent schools in our list?

Schools, Independent
  See **Independent Schools** *and* **Independent schools**
                                        x Schools, Independent
—turn to frame 151.

Independent schools
  See Schools, Independent *and* Schools, Independent
                                     x **Independent schools**
—turn to frame 158.

147 No.

The instruction
Universities
   xx **Higher education**
means make the reference:
Higher education
   See also **Universities**

Remember that references are always made *towards* a heading, and that consequently the instruction to create a reference will appear under the heading to which the reference will lead. Since the instruction we are considering appears under **Universities,** our reference will lead to **Universities.**

Try another example.

In an alphabetical list of subject headings what is meant by the instruction:
Overhead projectors
   xx **Audio-visual aids**
Make the reference:
Overhead projectors
   See also **Audio-visual aids**—turn to frame 144.
Make the reference:
Audio-visual aids
   See also **Overhead projectors**—turn to frame 160.

---

148 No, you are still wrong.

As between **Qualifications** and **Graduate** it is clear that the broader subject is **Qualifications,** a **Graduate** qualification being one kind of qualification. A downwards reference, from the broader subject to the narrower, would thus be:
Qualifications
   See also **Graduate**
Turn to frame 160 and re-consider this point

---

149 No, you are still wrong.

Once again you have mis-directed the indexer, away from the correct term towards the incorrect term. The point of the link is to act as a signpost, and we do not usually (unless as a deliberate act of sabotage!) cause a signpost to point in the wrong direction.

Turn to frame 128 and study this point carefully.

150 No, you are wrong.

You are mis-directing your user. You are instructing the indexer to refer the user *away* from the correct term! Remember, $x=$ ' refer from ', so x **Higher education**$=$' refer from **Higher education** ', whereas what we need is a reference *towards* **Higher education** from Tertiary education, *ie* x Tertiary education. This instruction should, therefore, appear under **Higher education,** viz:

Higher education
   x Tertiary education

What instruction should we provide as between Catholic and **Roman Catholic?**

Roman Catholic
   x Catholic—turn to frame 146.

Catholic
   x **Roman Catholic**—turn to frame 140.

---

151 Good, you are right.

Now examine the list of terms in frame 129 and insert all necessary *see* references and x instructions. Remember that we shall require a *see* reference from every unused term, and a corresponding x instruction under the appropriate used term. At this stage you should insert into the list the inverted construction of any term combinations (*eg* Primary education—Education, Primary) treating the inversion as an unused term.

You will find this list in frame 152. Study it, and then turn to frame 153.

152 The list is as follows:

Administration
Adults
Advanced level
   x Level, Advanced
Agents
Anglican schools
   See **Church of England schools**
Anthropology
Areas of slum housing
   See **Slum housing areas**
Arts subjects
   See **Humanities**
Audio-visual aids

Blind
Books
Boys

Catholic schools
   See **Roman Catholic schools**
Chairs
Chemistry
Children
Church of England schools
   x Anglican schools
     Schools, Anglican
     Schools, Church of England
Church schools
   x Schools, Church
Classrooms
Climbing frames
Comprehensive schools
   x Schools, Comprehensive
     Non-selective schools
     Schools, Non-selective
Country
   See **Rural**
Curriculum

Deaf
Desks
Domestic science
Dyslexia

Economics
Educands
   x Pupils; Students
Education, Elementary
   See **Primary education**
Education, Higher
   See **Higher education**
Education, Primary
   See **Primary education**
Education, Secondary
   See **Secondary education**
Education, Tertiary
   See **Higher education**
Elementary education
   See **Primary Education**
Elementary level
   x Level, Elementary
English language
English literature
English studies
Environment, Home
   See **Home environment**
Equipment

Facilities
Film-strips
Foreign languages
   x Languages
French
Furniture

German
Girls
Government schools
   See **State schools**
Graduate

Handicapped
Handicapped, Mentally
   See **Mentally handicapped**
Handicapped, Physically
   See **Physically handicapped**
Hearing

Higher education
   x Education, Higher;
     Education, Tertiary;
     Tertiary education
History
Home environment
   x Environment, Home
Humanities
   x Arts subjects

Immigrants
Independent schools
   x Schools, Independent;
     Public schools (British usage)
Inspectors

Laboratories
Languages
   See **Foreign languages**
Learning, Programmed
   See **Programmed learning**
Level, Elementary
   See **Elementary level**
Level, Advanced
   See **Advanced level**
Levels
Libraries

Marital status
Married
Mentally handicapped
   x Handicapped, Mentally
Methods of teaching
   See **Teaching methods**

Non-graduate
Non-selective schools
   See **Comprehensive schools**

Operations
Overhead projectors
   x Projectors, Overhead

Parents
Partially sighted

Part-time
Physical education
Physically handicapped
   x Handicapped, Physically
Playgrounds
Polytechnics
Popularization
Primary education
   x Education, Elementary;
     Education, Primary;
     Elementary education
Programmed learning
   x Learning, Programmed
Projectors, Overhead
   See **Overhead projectors**
Provision
Public schools
   See **Independent schools** (for
     British usage);
     State schools (for non-British
     usage)
Pupils
   See **Educands**
Purchase

Qualifications

Reading
Recruitment
Roman Catholic schools
   x Catholic schools;
     Schools, Catholic;
     Schools, Roman Catholic
Rural
   x Country

Schools
Schools, Anglican
   See **Church of England schools**
Schools, Catholic
   See **Roman Catholic schools**
Schools, Church
   See **Church schools**
Schools, Comprehensive
   See **Comprehensive schools**

152 (*cont*)

Schools, Government
  See **State schools**
Schools, Independent
  See **Independent schools**
Schools, Non-selective
  See **Comprehensive schools**
Schools, Public
  See **Independent schools** (for
    British usage);
    State schools (for non-British
    usage)
Schools, Roman Catholic
  See **Roman Catholic schools**
Schools, State
  See **State schools**
Secondary education
  x Education, Secondary
Selection
Sight
Social sciences
Sport
Staffing
State schools
  x Government schools;
    Public schools (non-British usage);
    Schools, Government; Schools,
    Public (non-British usage);
    Schools, State
Students
  See **Educands**
Subjects

Teachers
Teaching
Teaching aids
Teaching methods
  x Methods of teaching
Television
Terms of attendance
Tertiary education
  See **Higher education**

Universities

Video tapes

Women
Working class

153 We have now dealt with the problem of vocabulary control in an alphabetical list of subject headings. We have seen that it is important to ensure that, in the list itself, there is adequate guidance to ensure that the indexer using the list is guided, when necessary, *from* the approach vocabulary (unused terms and forms of construction) *to* the index vocabulary (used terms and forms of construction). We have seen also that it is necessary to provide instructions under some used terms and constructions designed to ensure that similar guidance will be provided in the index for the benefit of users. We can now turn to the problem of subject relationships between the various terms and constructions in the index vocabulary.

Subject relationships in a pre-coordinate alphabetical index are shown by means of *see also* references; in such an index a *see also* reference is intended to indicate to a user, who has been guided in his search to one place in the index, the possibility that relevant information might also be found at some other place indicated by the reference, *eg*:

Teaching methods
  See also **Popularization**
would be an indication to a user checking entries under **Teaching methods** that relevant information might also be found under the heading **Popularization.**

What would be indicated by the reference:

Higher education
  See also **Universities**

That information related to the subject of **Higher education** may also be found under the heading **Universities**—turn to frame 157.

That information related to the subject of **Universities** may also be found under the heading **Higher education**—turn to frame 141.

154 We can now enter in our list the instructions for downwards *see also* references. Remember that for each term we shall make an instruction to refer from the immediately superior term within the category, and the instruction is coded *xx, eg* :

Audio-visual aids
  xx **Teaching aids**

This instruction, under each appropriate term, will follow any *see* reference instructions (*x*).

Now do this for the terms in your alphabetical listing.

You will find the beginning of our alphabetical listing, with *xx* instructions added, in frame 155. Study it and then turn to frame 156.

155 The beginning of the list, with downwards *xx* instructions added, will be as follows:

Adminstration
  xx **Operations**
Adults
  xx **Educands**
Advanced level
  x **Level, Advanced**
  xx **Levels**
Agents
Anglican schools
  See **Church of England schools**
Anthropology
  xx **Science**
Areas of slum housing
  See **Slum housing areas**
Arts subjects
  See **Humanities**
Audio-visual aids
  xx **Teaching aids**

Blind
  xx **Sight**
Books
  xx **Teaching aids**
Boys
  xx **Children**

Catholic schools
  See **Roman Catholic schools**
Chairs
  xx **Furniture**
Chemistry
  xx **Science**
Children
  xx **Educands**
Church schools
  x **Schools, Church**
  xx **Schools**

Church of England schools
  x Anglican schools;
  Schools, Anglican;
  Schools, Church of England
  xx **Church schools**
Classrooms
  xx **Facilities**
Climbing frames
  xx **Teaching aids**
Comprehensive schools
  x Non-selective schools
  Schools, Comprehensive
  Schools, Non-selective
  xx **Schools**
Country
  See **Rural**
Curriculum

Deaf
  xx **Hearing**
Desks
  xx **Furniture**
Domestic science
  xx **Subjects**
Dyslexia
  xx **Mentally handicapped**

Economics
  xx **Social sciences**
Educands
  x Pupils; Students
Education, Elementary
  See **Primary education**
Education, Higher
  See **Tertiary education**
Education, Primary
  See **Primary education**
Education, Secondary
  See **Secondary education**

156 A second kind of *see also* reference is made between what are called coordinate subjects, that is subjects which are related to a common immediately superior subject. You may find it helpful to think of these as ' sideways ' references, they are usually referred to as *collateral* references.

Collateral references are not made between all coordinate subjects, but only when the two subjects are mutually illustrative or otherwise closely connected. For example, if we were making a subject headings list for the subject of Building, we would find a subcategory of *Rooms—Bedrooms, Kitchens, Lounges, Dining rooms, Bathrooms* etc. Of the terms listed here only *Kitchens* and *Dining rooms* need be linked by means of a collateral reference. Notice that the link is always made in both directions, *ie*:

Dining rooms	**Kitchens**
See also	*See also*
Kitchens	**Dining rooms**

Examine the basic analysis and insert collateral references as appropriate. Then turn to frame 161 where you will find part of our list with collateral references added. Study this and then turn to frame 162.

157 Good, you are quite right.

You will remember that references are made *towards* a heading, so the *instruction to the indexer* to make a reference will always appear under the heading *towards which* the reference is made, *ie* the instruction to make the reference

Teaching methods
   See also **Popularization**

will appear in our subject headings list under **Teaching methods.**

The code for the instruction is *xx*, so the instruction just referred to will appear as:

Popularization
   xx **Teaching methods**

xx **Teaching methods** being an instruction to the indexer to make a *see also* reference *from* **Teaching methods** *towards* (in this case) **Popularization.**

In an alphabetical list subject headings

Universities
   xx **Higher education**

is an instruction to make what reference?

Universities
   See also **Higher education**—turn to frame 147.
Higher education
   See also **Universities**—turn to frame 160.

158 No, you have confused the two sets of instructions.

Remember that we have adopted the uninverted construction of the combination as the used construction; this will, therefore, be rendered in bold type. Since this is the construction we have adopted for our index vocabulary, references will be *towards* it, because these references are intended to be used as signposts. So in the alphabetical list we require:

i) The inclusion of the rejected construction: Schools, Independent with a reference (signpost) to the adopted construction. This is for the benefit of the indexer.

Schools, Independent

See **Independent schools**

ii) Under **Independent schools** we need an instruction to the indexer that, when using the term in a heading, he should include *in the index* a reference (signpost) for the benefit of users who may look under the unused construction, guiding them to the used construction:

Independent schools

x Schools, Independent

Study this frame carefully, then try another example.

How should we treat Programmed learning in our list?

Programmed learning	*and*	Learning Programmed
See Learning, Programmed		x **Programmed learning**

—turn to frame 137.

Learning, Programmed	*and*	**Programmed learning**
See **Programmed learning**		x Learning, Programmed

—turn to frame 151.

159 No, this is quite wrong.

The correct downwards reference to **Chemistry** is from **Science**, the immediately superior term. You have ignored *two* intermediate steps in selecting **Curriculum—Subjects,** and **Science.** You have clearly not grasped the point.

In a structured alphabetical index there should be a network of downwards references which form, as it were, a ladder, leading from the most general subject in a hierarchy to the most special. The rungs of the ladder are the intermediate subjects, and the references connect the rungs one by one. Thus there should be a downwards reference from **Curriculum** to **Subjects,** from **Subjects** to **Science,** and from **Science** to **Chemistry**:

Curriculum	Subjects	Science
See also	*See also*	*See also*
Subjects	**Science**	**Chemistry**

Study this frame carefully, and then refer back to frame 145.

160 Good, you are making progress.

See also references are usually made between terms which belong to the same broad category. Such references may be 'downwards' or 'sideways'. We will consider first 'downwards' references.

It is customary in pre-coordinate alphabetical indexing to refer from a broader term to a narrower related term, for example from **Teaching methods** to **Programmed learning;** the diagram below illustrates the relationship:

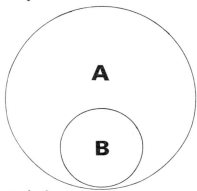

A = Teaching methods
B = Programmed learning

There is a hierarchical relationship between **Teaching methods** and the term within the category, as illustrated below.

Teaching methods

Popularization   Programmed learning

References are made from the broader subject to the narrower, or down the hierarchy.

Refer back to the analysis in frame 84 and decide how **Sport** and **Physical education** should be linked:

Physical education
 See also **Sport**—turn to frame 145.

Sport
 See also **Physical education**—turn to frame 127.

Administration
  xx **Operations**
Adults
  xx **Educands**
Advanced level
  x Level, Advanced
  xx **Levels**
Agents
Anglican schools
  See **Church of England schools**
Anthropology
  xx **Science**
Areas of slum housing
  See **Slum housing areas**
Arts subjects
  See **Humanities**
Audio-visual aids
  xx **Teaching aids**

Blind
  xx **Partially sighted; Sight**
Books
  xx **Teaching aids**
Boys
  xx **Children**

Catholic schools
  See **Roman Catholic schools**
Chairs
  xx **Furniture**
Chemistry
  xx **Science**
Children
  xx **Educands**
Church of England schools
  x Anglican schools;
    Schools, Anglican;
  Schools, Church of England
  xx **Church schools**

Church schools
  x Schools, Church
  xx **Schools**
Classrooms
  xx **Facilities; Laboratories**
Climbing frames
  xx **Teaching aids**
Comprehensive schools
  x Non-selective schools
    Schools, Comprehensive
    Schools, Non-selective
  xx **Schools**
Country
  See **Rural**
Curriculum

Deaf
  xx **Hearing**
Desks
  xx **Furniture**
Domestic science
  xx **Subjects**
Dyslexia
  xx **Mentally handicapped**

Economics
  xx **Social sciences**
Educands
  x Pupils; Students
Education, Elementary
  See **Primary education**
Education, Higher
  See **Higher education**
Education, Primary
  See **Primary education**
Education, Secondary
  See **Secondary education**

162 There is a very good case to be made for making *upwards* *see also* references as well as downwards, but alphabetical lists of subject headings do not usually make this provision in practice. For this reason we will not make such provision in our list.

It may be noted that, if we were to make this provison, *all* terms which are linked by *see also* references would be linked in both directions, not just those linked by collateral references.

Now turn to frame 164.

---

163 Good, you are right.

An exception to this rule arises in the case of steps of division which are *unsought, ie* they have been included in the analysis as a necessary step of division for producing a certain grouping of terms, but the concept has no literary warrant (*ie* it is not written about) and would not be used by a reader in formulating a search. Examples in our subject are: *Educational operations, Educational agents, Schools by owner, Schools by basis of selection,* and the headings for sub-categories of our **Educands** category with the exception of **Handicapped.** These terms have not been included in our alphabetical listing.

Where a step of division is unsought we may refer from the next superior term, *eg*:

Operations
   See also
   Teaching

not

Operations   Educational operations
   See also   &   *See also*
   Educational operations   Teaching

Now turn to frame 154.

164 The *see also* references which we have so far considered have all reflected relationships displayed in our basic analysis set out in frame 84. However, there is a further kind of *see also* reference which John Horner has styled ' oblique '[1]; these are references between terms from quite different categories. These are essentially intuitive as there is no way in which they can be revealed by the structure of our subject analysis. Notice also that, as with collateral references, the reference should be made in both directions. An example of two terms in our index language which might be linked in this way is **Science** and **Laboratories.** We should therefore provide the following instructions:

Science	**Laboratories**
xx **Laboratories**	*xx* **Science**

which will result in the following references respectively:

Laboratories	**Science**
See also	*See also*
Science	**Laboratories**

Examine the terms in frame 84 and see if you can identify any other pairs of terms, each of the pair being in a different category, which should be linked in this way. If you find any, make the necessary instructions. Then turn to frame 167.

[1] Horner, John: *Cataloguing,* AAL, 1970, p 107.

165 No·

The reference should be from the immediately superior term *ie* **Teaching aids.** The reference from **Equipment** would be to **Teaching aids,** not to **Audio-visual aids.** To proceed from **Equipment** to **Audio-visual aids** requires two steps, not one as you have supposed, *ie*

Equipment	**Teaching aids**
See also	*See also*
Teaching aids	**Audio-visual aids**

By proceeding directly from **Equipment** to **Audio-visual aids** you would conceal the relationship between **Teaching aids** and **Audio-visual aids.** There would be no link between the two, and the reader searching under **Teaching aids** would not be directed to the possibly related material entered under **Audio-visual aids.**

Try another example.

What downwards reference should be made to **Chemistry?**

Subjects

See also **Chemistry**—turn to frame 166.

Science

See also **Chemistry**—turn to frame 163.

Curriculum

See also **Chemistry**—turn to frame 159.

---

166 No.

You have made exactly the same mistake as before. The downwards reference to **Chemistry** should be from **Science;** you have omitted this step. **Science** is the immediately superior term, and if you decide that the downwards reference to **Chemistry** will be from **Subjects** you will have no downwards connecting link between **Science** and **Chemistry.**

This is a very important point which you must grasp clearly. Refer back to frame 145 and study it carefully.

167 It is usual, in an alphabetical list of subject headings, to indicate under each vocabulary term (*ie* each term adopted for use in headings) the narrower terms towards which references should be made from the term in question, *when the narrower term has been used as a heading*. Thus, since we have an instruction under **Audio-visual aids** to make a reference from **Teaching aids**, we should include a parallel note under **Teaching aids** that such a reference should exist if **Audio-visual aids** has been used as a heading. Such notes help to define the scope of a term, and may assist the indexer in his choice of heading.

Hence the note

Teaching aids
> *See also* **Audio-visual aids**

in our alphabetical list, is parallel with the instruction in the list:

Audio-visual aids
> *xx* **Teaching aids**

Every *xx* instruction in our list should have its parallel *see also* note.

These *see also* notes precede the *x* and *xx* instructions under each term, thus under any given term the sequence will be: i) *see also* note, ii) *x* instruction, iii) *xx* instruction.

Now insert *see also* notes into your list.

You will find the alphabetical listing, with all *see also* notes, *x* instructions, *xx* instructions, and see references from unused terms, in frame 168. Study it, and then turn to frame 169.

Administration
  See also **Provision; Staffing**
  xx **Operations**
Adults
  See also **Women**
  xx **Educands**
Advanced level
  x **Level, Advanced**
  xx **Levels**
Agents
  See also **Inspectors; Teachers**
Anglican schools
  See **Church of England schools**
Anthropology
  xx **Science**
Areas of slum housing
  xx **Slum housing areas**
Arts subjects
  See **Humanities**
Audio-visual aids
  See also **Film-strips;**
    Overhead projectors;
    Television; Video tapes
  xx **Teaching aids**

Blind
  See also **Partially sighted**
  xx **Partially sighted; Sight**
Books
  See also Libraries
  xx **Libraries; Teaching aids**
Boys
  xx **Children**

Catholic schools
  See **Roman Catholic schools**
Chairs
  xx **Furniture**
Chemistry
  xx **Science**
Children
  See also **Boys; Girls**
  xx **Educands**

Church of England schools
  x Anglican schools;
    Schools, Anglican;
    Schools, Church of England
  xx **Church schools**
Church schools
  x Schools, Church
  xx **Schools**
Classrooms
  See also **Laboratories**
  xx **Facilities; Laboratories**
Climbing frames
  xx **Teaching aids**
Comprehensive schools
  x Non-selective schools;
    Schools, Comprehensive;
    Schools, Non-selective
  xx **Schools**
Country
  See **Rural**
Curriculum
  xx **Levels; Subjects**

Deaf
  xx **Hearing**
Desks
  xx **Furniture**
Domestic science
  See also **Girls**
  xx **Girls; Subjects**
Dyslexia
  xx **Mentally handicapped**

Economics
  xx **Social sciences**
Educands
  See also **Adults; Children; Handi-**
    capped; Higher education; Im-
    migrants; Primary education;
    Secondary education; Social class
Education, Elementary
  See **Primary education**
Education, Higher
  See **Higher education**

168 (*cont*)

Education, Primary
  See **Primary education**
Education, Secondary
  See **Secondary education**
Education, Tertiary
  See **Higher education**
Elementary education
  See **Primary education**
Elementary level
  x Level, Elementary
  xx **Levels**
English language
  xx **English studies**
English literature
  xx **English studies**
English studies
  See also **English language; English
    literature**
Environment, Home
  See **Home environment**
Equipment
  See also **Furniture; Teaching aids**

Facilities
  See also **Classrooms; Laboratories;
    Libraries; Playgrounds**
Film-strips
  xx **Audio-visual aids**
Foreign languages
  See also **French; German**
  xx **Humanities**
French
  xx **Foreign languages**
Full-time
  xx **Terms of attendance**
Furniture
  See also **Chairs; Desks**
  xx **Equipment**
German
  xx **Foreign languages**
Girls
  xx **Children**
Government schools
  See **State schools**
Graduate
  xx **Qualifications**
  5

Handicapped
  See also **Immigrants; Mentally
    Handicapped; Physically handi-
    capped**
  xx **Educands; Immigrants**
Handicapped, Mentally
  See **Mentally handicapped**
Handicapped, Physically
  xx **Physically handicapped**
Hearing
  See also **Deaf**
  xx **Physically handicapped**
Higher education
  See also **Polytechnics; Universities**
  x Education, Higher;
    Education, Tertiary;
    Tertiary education
  xx **Educands**
History
  xx **Humanities**
Home environment
  See also **Parents**
  x Environment, Home
Humanities
  See also **English studies; Foreign
    languages; History**
  x Arts subjects
  xx **Subjects**

Immigrants
  See also **Handicapped**
  xx **Educands; Handicapped**
Independent schools
  x Schools, Independent;
    Private schools;
    Public schools (British usage)
  xx **Schools**
Inspectors
  xx **Agents**

Laboratories
  See also **Classrooms**
  xx **Facilities**
Languages
  See **Foreign languages**

Learning, Programmed
  See **Programmed learning**
Levels
  See also **Advanced level; Elementary level**
Libraries
  See also **Books**
  xx **Books; Facilities**
Marital status
  See also **Married**
  xx **Properties**
Married
  xx **Marital status**
Mentally handicapped
  See also **Dyslexia**
  x Handicapped, Mentally
  xx **Handicapped**
Methods of teaching
  See **Teaching methods**
Middle class
  xx **Social class**

Non-graduate
  xx Qualifications
Non-selective schools
  See **Comprehensive schools**

Operations
  See also **Administration; Teaching**
Overhead projectors
  x Projectors, Overhead
  xx **Audio-visual aids**

Parents
  xx **Home environment**
Partially sighted
  See also **Blind**
  xx **Blind; Sight**
Part-time
  xx **Terms of attendance**
Physical education
  See also **Sport**
  xx **Subjects**
Physically handicapped
  See also **Hearing; Sight**
  x Handicapped, Physically
  xx **Handicapped**

Playgrounds
  xx **Facilities**
Polytechnics
  xx **Higher education**
Popularization
  xx **Teaching methods**
Programmed learning
  x Learning, Programmed
  xx **Teaching methods**
Primary education
  x Education, Elementary
  Education, Primary
  Elementary education
  xx **Educands**
Private schools
  See **Independent schools**
Projectors, Overhead
  See **Overhead projectors**
Promotion
  xx **Staffing**
Properties
  See also **Marital status; Qualifications; Terms of attendance**
Provision
  See also **Purchase**
  xx **Administration**
Public schools
  See **Independent schools** (for British usage); **State schools** (for non-British usage)
Pupils
  See **Educands**
Purchase
  xx **Provision**

Qualifications
  See also **Graduate; Non-graduate**

Reading
  xx **Subjects**
Recruitment
  xx **Staffing**
Roman Catholic schools
  x Catholic schools;
  Schools, Catholic;

Schools, Roman Catholic
xx **Church schools**
Rural
x Country

Schools
See also **Church schools; Comprehensive schools; Independent schools; State schools**
Schools, Anglican
See **Church of England schools**
Schools, Catholic
See **Roman Catholic schools**
Schools, Church
See **Church schools**
Schools, Church of England
See **Church of England schools**
Schools, Comprehensive
See **Comprehensive schools**
Schools, Government
See **State schools**
Schools, Independent
See **Independent schools**
Schools, Non-selective
See **Comprehensive schools**
Schools, Private
See **Independent schools**
Schools, Public
See **Independent schools** (British usage); **State schools** (non-British usage)
Schools, Roman Catholic
See **Roman Catholic schools**
Schools, State
See **State schools**
Science
See also **Anthropology; Chemistry**
xx **Subjects**
Secondary education
x Education, Secondary
xx **Educands**
Selection
Sight
See also **Blind; Partially sighted**

Slum housing areas
x Areas of slum housing
xx **Urban**
Social class
See also **Middle class; Working class**
Social sciences
See also **Economics**
xx **Subjects**
Sport
xx **Physical education**
Staffing
See also **Promotion; Recruitment**
xx **Administration**
State schools
x **Government schools;** Public schools (non-British usage); Schools, Government; Schools, State
xx **Schools**
Students
See **Educands**
Subjects
See also **Domestic science; Humanities; Physical education; Reading; Science; Social sciences**

Teachers
xx **Agents**
Teaching
xx **Operations**
Teaching aids
See also **Audio-visual aids; Books; Climbing frames**
xx **Equipment**
Teaching methods
See also **Popularization; Programmed learning**
x Methods of teaching
Television
See also **Video tapes**
xx **Audio-visual aids; Video tapes**
Terms of attendance
See also **Full-time; Part-time**
Tertiary education
See **Higher education**

Universities
  xx **Higher education**
Urban
  See also **Slum housing areas**

Video tapes
  See also **Television**
  xx **Audio-visual aids; Television**

Women
  xx **Adults**
Working class
  xx **Social class**

---

169 It is usual to list common sub-divisions in a separate sequence at the front of the main list. You will find this, for example, in Sears *List of subject headings.* There is, in Sears, an accompanying instruction that the terms in the list may be added at certain points, as indicated after each term; we shall require an instruction that these terms may be added *at the end* of any heading constructed from terms in the main list, and that if terms are used from both the list of *Common subjects* and the list of *Forms of presentation,* the former should take precedence.

We can now add the list of *Common subjects and* the list of *Forms of presentation,* together with the necessary instructions.

Turn to frame 170.

---

170 You have probably noticed that we have not yet made any provision for terms in the Geo-political Place or Time categories. In an alphabetical list of subject headings it is the usual practice not to list names of places (or persons), but to provide an instruction that the indexer may add these at will. We can do the same for the Time category, stipulating that these be always added in the form of *dates, ie not 19th century,* but 1801-1900, and so on. In this way we can obviate possible filing problems. This section, of *Terms to be supplied by the indexer,* will precede the list of common sub-divisions.

We can now add this section to our list.

Now turn to frame 171.

171 The final step in constructing an alphabetical list of subject headings will be to write an Introduction, including instructions on how to use the list, and examples of headings constructed from the terms in the list. It should also, for a synthetic list, include the combination order, and an explanation of how this works.

Since the alphabetical listing is completely unsystematic, the combination order will bear no relationship to the order in which the terms are listed *ie* categories of terms are scattered at the whim of the alphabetical order, and it will not be apparent from the order which category any term belongs to. It will, therefore, be necessary to code each category and sub-category, for example with a number, repeating that number against the appropriate terms in the alphabetical list. In this way the indexer will be able to identify the category or sub-category to which each term belongs, and using the code will be able to assemble the terms in a compound heading in the correct order. If our code signs have ordinal value, and the sign having the highest ordinal value is allocated to the primary sub-category, and so on, then when the indexer has assembled the terms for a particular heading their combination will be straightforward, following the ordinal value of the code. For example :

Advanced level (8)
Chemistry (7)
Film-strips (13)
Teaching (9)

produces the heading :

Chemistry : Advanced : level : Teaching : Film-strips

The *Introduction* will also need to give instructions on the punctuation to be used between terms in compound headings. As you will notice above we have adopted the colon. This is an arbitrary decision, a hyphen or a comma would do equally as well.

Turn now to frame 172.

172 In an alphabetical list of subject headings the combination order has the effect of collocating headings relating to our primary category, since when terms from that category are used in a heading they will be given precedence and the resulting heading will file under that term. For example the subject of *Science in State primary schools in Victoria* will file under *Primary education, ie*:

Primary education: Science: State schools: Victoria

But the user of the index may not be acquainted with the combination order, and may well look for this subject under *Science,* or *State schools,* or even *Victoria.* We therefore need a system of references to guide him to the correct place in the event that he refers to a subordinated term. One convenient way of doing this is to drop terms successively from the front of the heading, *ie*:

Science: State schools: Victoria

See also **Primary education: Science: State schools: Victoria**
State schools: Victoria

See also **Science: State schools: Victoria**
Victoria

See also **State schools: Victoria**

Such a system of references will ensure that, whatever constituent term a reader refers to, he will be led to the correct entry. Instructions on this must be included in the *Introduction.*

Please turn to frame 173.

---

173 Our alphabetical list of subject headings is now complete. You are making good progress with the programme, and probably deserve a break. If you wish to take a rest from your study of the programme this is a suitable point at which to take it. You can resume with the next paragraph.

We have now utilized our basic analysis as the basis of two different kinds of pre-coordinate structured index language: a classification scheme, and an alphabetical list of subject headings. We can also use it as a basis of a different kind of structured index language: a post-coordinate system.

Please turn to frame 174.

174 A *post-coordinate* index language is one which includes only terms representing a single concept, with no provision for their combination by the indexer to specify compound subjects. In a post-coordinate index the terms necessary to specify a compound subject are brought together (co-ordinated) by the user after (post) the search. For example, if a user requires information on *Science in Australian Universities* he will locate in the index the three terms which together specify the subject, viz **Science; Australia; Universities.** On each of the cards thus located will be a list of documents (usually by accession number) whose subject description includes the term in question. A document common to all three cards will be a document on the subject in question.

eg

Suppose that under each term we have the following numbers:

Science	57	296	471	693	714	839	985
Australia	64	178	194	296	839	985	991
Universities	78	296	307	471	714	792	817

Document number 296 will be on the subject *Science in Australian Universities.* Document number 471, however, is on *Science in the University* (*ie* it is not specifically related to Australia).

What are the essential features of post-coordinate systems?

Turn to frame 175.

---

175 You should have answered that the essential features of post-coordinate systems are that entries are made for single concepts only, and that these are coordinated *after* the search to specify compound subjects. If your answer was significantly different you should study frame 174 again carefully, before proceeding.

Because a post-coordinate system does not attempt to make provision for the combination of simple subjects there are no problems of combination order, which is concerned essentially with the order of terms in a compound heading. The only subject analysis we need is the basic analysis as set out in frame 84.

Why do we not need a combination order in a post-coordinate index language?

Turn to frame 176.

176 You should have answered that we do not require a combination order since this is concerned with the order of terms in a compound heading, whereas a post-coordinate system indexes only single concepts.

Our first concern will be to make an alphabetical list of terms. We could make two separate lists: one of approach terms and one of index vocabulary terms, but as it is more usual to consolidate the two we will have a single list including both. In order to distinguish between them we will put our index terms in **bold** type.

Why is it necessary to put index terms in bold type?

Turn to frame 177.

---

177 Index terms will be in **bold** type in order to distinguish them from approach terms.

Before we can make our list we should first check our terms to ensure that they can meaningfully stand alone. Normally a list of terms for a post-coordinate system includes single terms; however, term combination may be included where a term on its own is ambiguous or where ordinary usage would require this, so long as only one concept is involved.

Check our list of terms (it is set out conveniently in frame 84) to see whether any term combinations are required. Some of the simple concepts listed are already identified by term combinations and these combinations may be included in our list. Make a list of any others you identify.

Turn to frame 178.

178 The following is a list of terms which might be used in combination:

Advanced level
Church of England schools
Church schools
Comprehensive schools
Elementary level
English language
English literature
English studies
Higher education
Independent schools
Primary education
Roman Catholic schools   ,
Secondary education
State schools

Note that the thesaurus should include the inverted form of such combinations in the approach vocabulary, so that the user looking for, for example, *Education, Secondary*, may be guided to the correct form of the combination.

Why do we need to include, in the approach vocabulary, the inverted form of term combinations?

Turn to frame 179.

---

179 We need to include the inverted form of term combinations because a user of the index may look for this form rather than the one we have adopted.

The approach vocabulary will also include all synonyms and antonyms, and also single terms such as *Girls* which stand for complex (*ie* multi-aspect) concepts.

Now compile a single alphabetical list of all approach terms and index vocabulary terms, remembering that index vocabulary terms should be in **bold** type (on a typewriter, index vocabulary terms may conveniently be rendered in CAPITALS).

A list of terms for our system will be found in frame 180. Study this list, and then turn to frame 181.

180 The list is as follows:

Administration
Adults
Advanced level
Agents
Anglican schools
Anthropology
Areas of slum housing
Arts subjects
Audio-visual aids

Blind
Books

Catholic schools
Chairs
Chemistry
Children
Church of England
   schools
Church schools
Classrooms
Climbing frames
Comprehensive schools
Country
Curriculum

Deaf
Desks
Domestic science
Dyslexia

Economics
Educands
Education, Elementary
Education, Higher
Education, Primary
Education, Tertiary
Elementary education
Elementary level
English language
English literature
English studies
Equipment

Facilities
Film-strips
Foreign languages
French
Furniture

German
Government schools
Graduates

Handicapped
Handicapped, Mentally
Handicapped, Physically
Hearing
History
Home environment
Humanities

Immigrants
Independent schools
Inspectors

Laboratories
Languages
Learning, Programmed
Levels
Libraries

Marital status
Married
Mentally handicapped
Methods of teaching

Non-graduate
Non-selective schools

Operations
Overhead projectors

Parents
Partially sighted
Part-time
Physical education

Physically handicapped
Playgrounds
Polytechnics
Popularization
Primary education
Programmed learning
Projectors, Overhead
Promotion
Properties
Provision
Public schools
Pupils
Purchase

Qualifications

Reading
Recruitment
Roman Catholic schools
Rural

Schools
Schools, Catholic
Schools, Church
Schools, Comprehensive
Schools, Government
Schools, Independent
Schools, Public
Schools, Roman Catholic
Schools, State
Secondary education
Selection
Sight
Slum housing areas
Social sciences
Sport
Staffing
State schools
Students
Subjects

Teachers
Teaching
Teaching aids

180 (*cont*)

Teaching methods		Women
Television	Video tapes	Working class
Terms of attendance	Vocabulary	
Tertiary education	Universities	

---

181 The approach vocabulary is included so as to direct the user of a thesaurus to the correct index vocabulary term. The guidance takes the form of a USE instruction, equivalent to a *see* reference in an alphabetical list of subject headings, *eg*:

Non-selective schools
   USE **Comprehensive schools**

It will be necessary to provide such an instruction for each term in the approach vocabulary.

What form of instruction should we provide for ' Tertiary education ' and **Higher education**?

Tertiary education
   USE **Higher education**—turn to frame 189.
Higher education
   USE Tertiary education—turn to frame 185.

---

182 No, you have made the same mistake again.

The purpose of a USE instruction is to guide the user of a thesaurus from an unused term to the correct used term, which is featured in bold type. The instruction should, therefore, lead from the unfeatured (ordinary type) term to the featured (bold type) term, *ie*:

Arts
   USE **Humanities**

Consider this carefully, then turn to frame 181 and work through it again.

183 No, you have linked the two terms incorrectly.

USED FOR indicates that a vocabulary term, *ie* a used term which is therefore featured in bold type, stands for certain unused terms. The note accordingly appears under the used term, but you have put it under the unused term.

How will **Educands** and Students be linked by a USED FOR note?

Educands

USED FOR Students—turn to frame 193.

Students

USED FOR **Educands**—turn to frame 191.

---

184 No, you are still wrong.

You have made exactly the same mistake again. Of the two terms **Teaching methods** is the broader, and the BT note should, therefore, appear under **Programmed learning**.

Turn to frame 195 and work through this phase of the programme again.

---

185 No, you are wrong.

The purpose of a USE instruction is to guide the user of a thesaurus from an approach term, which has not been adopted for use in the index, to the correct used term. **Higher education** is a used term—it is featured in bold type. We should, therefore, be guiding the indexer to this term, not away from it; *ie* the instruction should be

Tertiary education

USE **Higher education**

What instruction should we provide for Arts and **Humanities**?

Humanities

USE Arts—turn to frame 182.

Arts

USE **Humanities**—turn to frame 189.

186 No, you have made the same mistake again.

Foreign languages is the wider term, and **French** the narrower; the concept of foreign languages includes all individual foreign languages. Consequently the NT note should appear under **Foreign languages**, the wider term:

Foreign languages
    NT **French**

Turn to frame 190 and work through it again.

---

187 No, you are wrong.

Of the two terms **Science** is the broader, and the concept of Science *includes* the concepts of Chemistry. The BT note will, therefore, appear under **Chemistry**.

Chemistry
    BT **Science**

Try another example

Teaching methods
    BT **Programmed learning**—turn to frame 184.

Programmed learning
    BT **Teaching methods**—turn to frame 190.

---

188 You should have replied that a NT note indicates a term narrower than the term under which it appears, and which is wholly included within the latter.

Consider the relationship between **Audio-visual aids** and **Overhead projectors**. How would this be shown by an NT note?

Audio-visual aids
    NT **Overhead projectors**—turn to frame 197.

Overhead projectors
    NT **Audio-visual aids**—turn to frame 192.

189 Good, you are correct.

Corresponding with these USE instructions are USED FOR notes under the appropriate used terms. These provide an indication of unused terms which are represented by the term in question, *eg*:

Comprehensive schools

USED FOR Non-selective schools

These notes will always appear under a term featured in bold type, and the terms following the USED FOR will always be in normal type.

How will Arts and **Humanities** be linked by a USED FOR note?
Arts

USED FOR **Humanities**—turn to frame 183.

Humanities

USED FOR Arts—turn to frame 193.

---

190 Good, you are right.

The converse of the BT note is NT.

NT = Narrower term—*ie* a term which denotes a concept narrower than the term under which the note appears, and which is included within the latter term, *eg*

Mentally handicapped =

NT **Dyslexia**

What is the meaning of a NT note?
Turn to frame 188.

---

191 No, you have made the same mistake again.

It is quite fundamental that a USED FOR note should appear under the used term. Work carefully through frame 189 again, and then attempt the question at the foot of that frame once more.

192 No, you are wrong.

The narrower term is **Overhead projectors**, and the NT note should therefore, appear under **Audio-visual aids**.

Audio-visual aids

ie

NT **Overhead projectors**

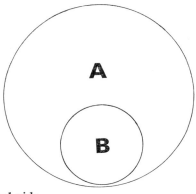

A = Audio-visual aids
B = Overhead projectors

Try another example.

Consider the relationship between **Foreign languages** and **French**. How would this be shown by an NT note?

Foreign languages
NT **French**—turn to frame 197.

French
NT **Foreign languages**—turn to frame 186.

193 Good, you are right.

We can now insert USE instructions and USED FOR notes into our list. Notice that usually each USE instruction will have a corresponding USED FOR note. The exception will be terms such as *Girls* which are represented in the index vocabulary by two separate terms. In such a case the instruction will read :

Girls

    USE **Children** and **Females**

and there will be no corresponding USED FOR note under the two index terms.

Now insert USE instructions and USED FOR notes.

You will find the alphabetical listing, with these instructions and notes inserted in frame 194. Study it and compare the list with your work, and then turn to frame 195.

194 The list is as follows:

Administration
Adults
Advanced level
Agents
Anglican schools
  USE Church of England schools
Anthropology
Areas of slum housing
  USE Slum housing areas
Arts subjects
  USE Humanities
Audio-visual aids

Blind
Books

Catholic schools
  USE Roman Catholic schools
Chairs
Chemistry
Children
Church of England Schools
  USED FOR Anglican schools
Church schools
  USED FOR Non-selective schools
             Schools, Comprehensive
Classroom,
Climbing frames
Comprehensive schools
  USED FOR Non-selective schools;
             Schools, comprehensive
Country
  USED FOR Rural

Deaf
Desks
Domestic science
Dyslexia

Economics
Educands
  USED FOR Pupils; Students
  6*

Education, Elementary
  USE Elementary education
Education, Higher
  USE Higher education
Education, Primary
  USE Primary education
Education, Secondary
  USE Secondary education
Education, Tertiary
  USE Higher education
Elementary education
  USE Primary education
Elementary level
English language
English literature
English studies
Equipment

Facilities
Film-strips
Foreign languages
  USED FOR Languages
French
Furniture

German
Government schools
  USE State schools
Graduates

Handicapped
Handicapped, Mentally
  USE Mentally handicapped
Handicapped, Physically
  USE Physically handicapped
Hearing
Higher education
  USED FOR Education, Higher
             Education, Tertiary
             Tertiary education
History
Home environment
Humanities
  USED FOR Arts subjects

Immigrants
Independent schools
USED FOR Schools, Independent
                Public schools (British
                usage)
Inspectors

Laboratories
Languages
USE Foreign languages
Learning, Programmed
USE Programmed learning
Levels
Libraries

Marital status
Married
Mentally handicapped
USED FOR Handicapped, Mentally
Methods of teaching
USE Teaching methods

Non-graduate
Non-selective schools
USE Comprehensive schools

Operations
Overhead projectors
USED FOR Projectors, Overhead

Parents
Partially sighted
Part-time
Physically handicapped
USED FOR Handicapped, Physically
Playgrounds
Polytechnics
Popularization
Primary education
USED FOR Education, Elementary
                Education, Primary
                Elementary education
Programmed Learning
USED FOR Learning, Programmed

Projectors, Overhead
USE Overhead projectors
Promotion
Properties
Provision
Public schools
USE Independent schools (for
                British usage);
                State schools (for non-British
                usage)
Pupils
USE Educands
Purchase

Qualification

Reading
Recruitment
Roman Catholic schools
USED FOR Catholic schools
                Schools, Catholic
                Schools, Roman Catholic
Rural

Schools
Schools, Catholic
USE Roman Catholic schools
Schools, Church
USE Church schools
Schools, Comprehensive
USE Comprehensive schools
Schools, Government
USE State schools
Schools, Independent
USE Independent schools
Schools, Public
USE Independent schools (for
                British usage)
                State schools (for non-British
                usage)
Schools, Roman Catholic
USE Roman Catholic schools
Schools, State
USE State schools

194 (*cont*)

Secondary education
 USED FOR Education, Secondary
Selection
Sight
Slum housing areas
 USED FOR Areas of slum housing
Sport
Staffing
State schools
 USED FOR Government schools
          Public schools (non-
           British usage)
          Schools, Government
          Schools, Public (non-
           British usage
Students
 USE **Educands**

Teachers
Teaching
Teaching aids
Teaching methods
 USED FOR Methods of teaching
Television
Terms of attendance
Tertiary education
 USE **Higher education**

Universities

Video tapes
Vocabulary

Women
Working class

---

195 Relationships in a thesaurus are indicated by means of BT, NT, and RT notes

BT = Broader term—*ie* a term which denotes a concept broader than the term under which the note appears, and which includes the latter term, *eg*

Dyslexia
 BT **Mentally handicapped**
What is the meaning of a BT *note*?
Turn to frame 196.

---

196 You should have replied that a BT note indicates a term wider than the term under which it appears, and which wholly includes the latter.

Consider the relationship between **Science** and **Chemistry**. How would this be shown by a BT note?

Science
 BT **Chemistry**—turn to frame 187.
Chemistry
 BT **Science**—turn to frame 190.

197 Good, you are quite right.

A very important principle to observe in making BT and NT notes is that terms which are connected in this way should be proximate, *ie* steps of division must not be omitted. For example we cannot have the following notes:

Humanities
  NT **French**

French
  BT **Humanities**

because this omits the intermediate step of division represented by Foreign languages. We should proceed:

Humanities
  NT **Foreign languages**

French
  BT **Foreign languages**

Foreign languages
  NT **French**

Foreign languages
  BT **Humanities**

If we omit the intermediate step, then users of our system may miss relevant information.

What steps will be necessary to lead by NT notes, from **Equipment** to **Television**?

Turn to frame 198.

---

198 You should have replied as follows:

Equipment
  NT **Audio-visual aids**   *not*

Equipment
  NT **Television**

Audio-visual aids
  NT **Television**

If you had the correct answer turn to frame 200; if not, read on.

If we fail to indicate the intermediate step of **Audio-visual aids,** then users of our system may miss relevant information through not being directed to this term. It is therefore most important that our system of BT and NT notes, which forms an important element in the network by which we indicate relationships should be carefully constructed to lead step by step from one term to the next.

What steps will be necessary to link **Subjects** and **Chemistry** by means of NT references? Turn to frame 199.

199 You should have replied as follows:
Subjects
  NT **Science**   *not*
Subjects
  NT **Chemistry**
Science
  NT **Chemistry**

If you had the correct answer turn to frame 200; if not turn to frame 195 and work through it again.

200 The third kind of note is an RT note.

RT = Related term.

This is used to indicate related terms which are co-ordinate (*ie* equal in status or specificity) with the term under which the note appears. Not all co-ordinate terms are indicated under an RT note, but only those which are co-ordinate *and* illustrative. Consider, for example, the relationships in the following diagram, where the circle comprises the category of ROOMS in an index language for the subject BUILDING.

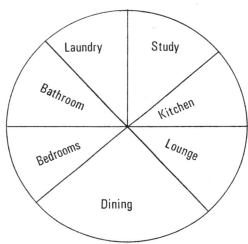

Under **Dining Room** we would probably have RT notes for **Kitchen** and **Lounge**, but not for **Bedrooms**, **Bathroom**, etc. RT notes should be made in both directions, *eg*:

Dining Room
   RT **Kitchen**
      Lounge

and

Kitchen   **Lounge**
   RT **Dining Room**   RT **Dining Room**

What RT notes would be necessary for **Partially-sighted**?

Turn to frame 201.

201 There is only one term co-ordinate with **Partially-sighted,** and that is **Blind.** Since this is an illustrative term (*ie* material on the education of blind persons might contain information relevant to a search for information in the education of partially-sighted persons) we should make an RT note.

Partially sighted
  RT **Blind**

Remember that this means that we must also make a corresponding note under **Blind**:

Blind
  RT **Partially-sighted**

Now go through your list and check each used term against the analysis in frame 84. Establish what other terms are related to it and make BT, NT, and RT notes as appropriate. Under each term there will follow an USED FOR note, and will appear in the order just cited.

When you have done this turn to frame 202 where you will find the complete list of terms with notes added. Study this and then turn to frame 203.

Administration
  BT **Operations**
  NT **Provision**
    Staffing
Adults
  BT **Educands**
Advanced level
  BT **Levels**
Agents
  NT **Inspectors**
    Teachers
Anglican schools
  USE **Church of England schools**
Anthropology
  BT **Science**
Areas of slum housing
  USE **Slum housing areas**
Arts subjects
  USE **Humanities**
Audio-visual aids
  BT **Teaching aids**
  NT **Film-strips**
    Overhead projectors
    Television
    Video tapes

Blind
  BT **Sight**
  RT **Partially sighted**
Books
  BT **Teaching aids**
  RT **Libraries**
Boys
  BT **Educands**
  RT **Children**

Catholic schools
  USE **Roman Catholic schools**
Chairs
  BT **Furniture**
Chemistry
  BT **Science**
Children
  BT **Educands**
Church of England Schools

  USED FOR Anglican schools
    Schools, Anglican
    Schools, Church of England
  BT **Church schools**
Church schools
  USED FOR Schools, Church
  BT **Schools**
Classrooms
  BT **Facilities**
  RT **Laboratories**
Climbing frames
  BT **Teaching aids**
Comprehensive schools
  USED FOR Non-selective schools
    Schools, Comprehensive
  BT **Schools**
Country
  USE **Rural**
Curriculum
  NT **Levels**
    Subjects

Deaf
  BT **Hearing**
Desks
  BT **Furniture**
Domestic science
  BT **Subjects**
Dyslexia
  BT **Mentally handicapped**

Economics
  BT **Social sciences**
Educands
  USED FOR Pupils; Students
  NT **Adults**
    Children
    Handicapped
    Higher education
    Immigrants
    Primary education
    Secondary education
    Social class
Education, Elementary
  USE **Primary education**

Education, Higher
  USE **Higher education**
Education, Primary
  USE **Primary education**
Education, Secondary
  USE **Secondary education**
Education, Tertiary
  USE **Higher education**
Elementary education
  USE **Primary education**
Elementary level
  BT **Levels**
English language
  BT **English studies**
English literature
  BT **English studies**
English studies
  NT **English language**
    English literature
  BT **Humanities**
Equipment
  NT **Furniture**
    Teaching aids

Facilities
  NT **Classrooms**
    Laboratories
    Libraries
    Playground
Film-strips
  BT **Audio-visual aids**
Foreign languages
  USED FOR Languages
  BT **Humanities**
  NT **French, German**
French
  BT **Foreign languages**
Full-time
  BT **Terms of attendance**
Furniture
  BT **Equipment**
  NT **Chairs**
    Desks

German
  BT **Foreign languages**

Girls
  BT **Educands**
  RT **Children**
Government schools
  USE **State schools**
Graduate
  BT **Qualifications**

Handicapped
  BT **Educands**
  NT **Mentally handicapped**
    Physically handicapped
  RT **Immigrants**
Handicapped, Mentally
  USE **Mentally handicapped**
Handicapped, Physically
  USE **Physically handicapped**
Hearing
  BT **Physically handicapped**
  NT **Deaf**
Higher education
  USED FOR Education, Higher
    Education, Tertiary
    Tertiary education
  BT **Educands**
  NT **Polytechnics**
    Universities
History
  BT **Humanities**
Home environment
  NT **Parents**
Humanities
  USED FOR Arts subjects
  BT **Subjects**
  NT **English studies**
    Foreign languages
    History

Immigrants
  BT **Educands**
  RT **Handicapped**
Independent schools
  USED FOR Public schools (British
    usage)
    Schools, Independent
  BT **Schools**

Inspectors
  BT **Agents**

Laboratories
  BT **Facilities**
Languages
  USE **Foreign languages**
Learning, Programmed
  USE **Programmed learning**
Levels
  NT **Advanced level**
      Elementary level
Libraries
  BT **Facilities**
  RT **Books**

Marital status
  BT **Properties**
  NT **Married**
Married
  BT **Marital status**
Mentally handicapped
  USED FOR Handicapped, Mentally
  BT **Handicapped**
  NT **Dyslexia**
Methods of teaching
  USE **Teaching methods**
Middle class
  BT **Social class**

Non-graduate
  BT **Qualifications**
Non-selective schools
  USE **Comprehensive schools**

Operations
  NT **Administration**
      Teaching
Overhead projectors
  USED FOR Projectors, Overhead
  BT **Audio-visual aids**

Parents
  BT **Home environment**
Partially sighted
  BT **Sight**
  RT **Blind**
Part-time
  BT **Terms of attendance**

Physical education
  BT **Subjects**
  NT **Sport**
Physically handicapped
  USED FOR Handicapped, Physically
  BT **Handicapped**
  NT **Hearing**
      Sight
Playgrounds
  BT **Facilities**
Polytechnics
  BT **Higher education**
Popularization
  BT **Teaching methods**
Programmed learning
  USED FOR Learning, Programmed
  BT **Teaching methods**
Primary education
  USED FOR Education, Elementary
      Education, Primary
      Elementary education
  BT **Educands**
Projectors, Overhead
  USE **Overhead projectors**
Promotion
  BT **Staffing**
Properties
  NT **Marital status**
     Qualifications
     Terms of attendance
Provision
  BT **Administration**
  NT **Purchase**
Public schools
  USE **Independent schools** (for
      British usage);
      State schools (for non-British
      usage)
Pupils
  USE **Educands**
Purchase
  BT **Provision**

Qualifications
  NT **Graduate**
     Non-graduate

Reading
  BT **Subjects**
Recruitment
  BT **Staffing**
Roman Catholic schools
  USED FOR Catholic schools
         Schools, Catholic
         Schools, Roman Catholic
  BT **Church schools**
Rural
  USED FOR Country

Schools
  NT **Church schools**
     Comprehensive schools
     Independent schools
     State schools
Schools, Anglican
  USE **Church of England schools**
Schools, Catholic
  USE **Roman Catholic schools**
Schools, Church
  USE **Church schools**
Schools, Church of England
  USE **Church of England schools**
Schools, Comprehensive
  USE **Comprehensive schools**
Schools, Government
  USE **State schools**
Schools, Independent
  USE **Independent schools**
Schools, Public
  USE **Independent schools** (for
         British usage)
     State schools (for non-British
         usage)
Schools, Roman Catholic
  USE **Roman Catholic schools**
Schools, State
  USE **State schools**
Science
  BT **Subjects**
  NT **Anthropology**
     Chemistry
Secondary education
  USED FOR Education, Secondary

  BT **Educands**
Selection
Sight
  BT **Physically handicapped**
  NT **Blind; Partially sighted**
Social class
  BT **Educands**
  NT **Middle class**
     Working class
Social sciences
  BT **Subjects**
  NT **Economics**
Sport
  BT **Physical education**
Staffing
  BT **Administration**
  NT **Promotion**
     Recruitment
State schools
  USED FOR Government schools
         Public schools (non-
             British usage)
         Schools, Government
         Schools, Public (non-
             British usage
  BT **Schools**
Students
  USE **Educands**
Subjects
  BT **Curriculum**
  NT **Domestic science**
     Humanities
     Physical education
     Reading
     Science
     Social science

Teachers
  BT **Agents**
Teaching
  BT **Operations**
Teaching aids
  BT **Equipment**
  NT **Audio-visual aids**
     Books
     Climbing frames

202 (*cont*)

Teaching methods
  USED FOR Methods of teaching
  NT **Popularization**
    Programmed learning
Television
  BT **Audio-visual aids**
  RT **Video tapes**
Terms of attendance
  NT **Full-time**
    Part-time
Tertiary education
  USE **Higher education**

Universities
  BT **Higher education**

Urban
  NT **Areas of slum housing**

Video tapes
  BT **Audio-visual aids**
  RT **Television**
Vocabulary

Women
  BT **Educands**
  RT **Adults**
Working class
  BT **Social class**

---

203 It remains to add two features:

a) A section: *Terms to be supplied by the indexer.*

This should indicate that terms in certain categories, (Geopolitical place, and Time) should be supplied by the indexer, and also names of persons and institutions.

b) An introduction which should explain the scope of the thesaurus, and provide clear instructions on how to use it.

This completes our thesaurus, and you may like to apply it to some of the titles in frame 5.

Then turn to frame 204.

204 Congratulations! You have now completed the programme.

The techniques which you have been studying can be applied to any subject field, from Literature to Nuclear physics. The theory was first formulated by the late Dr S R Ranganathan in his *Colon Classification,* and in various writings. He devoted his main attention to classification, and adopted a terminology which is now widely used. This terminology has been avoided in this programme because it is so closely identified with classification theory, whereas the intention of the programme has been to emphasize that the techniques may be applied to any structured index language. One of the basic terms coined by Ranganathan was *facet,* now widely used. A facet is the list of terms produced when a class is divided by a single characteristic of division; we have used the term *category* in the programme. Each term or concept within a facet is called a *focus.*

It is hoped that this programme will have given you an insight into the principles of subject analysis as they may be applied to the construction of a structured index language. Such an insight will be of use to you not only if you are faced with the task of compiling such an index language, but also in using and evaluating working systems.

If you wish to test your newly gained knowledge, a short test paper, with answers, follows.

SELF TEST

THERE FOLLOWS A SERIES of questions, each accompanied by a number of alternative statements, only one of which is wholly correct. Examine each question in turn, and make a note of the statement which you think is correct. Then turn to frame 206 and check your answers.

1 A structured index language is one which:

a) Attempts to indicate relationships between terms.

b) Specifies compound subjects by enumeration rather than by synthesis.

c) Employs a fixed citation order.

d) Has its terms arranged in a systematic order.

2 By literary warrant we mean that:

a) The allocation of terms between the index vocabulary and the approach vocabulary is based on a survey of the literature.

b) The terms used in the system are restricted to those found in the collection for which it is designed.

c) The initial choice of terms is based on a survey of the literature.

d) The performance of the system has been tested against a collection of documents.

3 In one of the following titles the term in italics represents a compound concept:

a) The role of the *churches* in modern education.

b) *English language* in primary schools.

c) Domestic science for *bachelors*.

d) Science in the polytechnics.

4 In index language construction, subject analysis is the process by which we establish:

a) The categories to be recognized, and their scope.

b) The terms to be included in the index vocabulary.

c) The scope of the subject to be covered by the system.

d) The schedules of a classification scheme.

5 If a broad category includes a number of terms which are not mutually exclusive, we must proceed with further division to establish sub-categories. This is essential to ensure that we:

a) Achieve complete hospitality.

b) Achieve specificity in the indexing of compound subjects.

c) Achieve modulation in displaying relationships.

d) Achieve predictability in indexing compound subjects.

6 Combination order is the order in which:

a) The terms are listed within each category or sub-category.

b) Terms are assembled to specify a compound subject.

c) The categories are listed in the schedules of a classification scheme.

d) The terms are listed in the basic analysis.

7 The principle of inversion must be observed if we wish to:

a) Ensure that the final order produced by applying a classification scheme will place the primary category first.

b) Ensure that a classification collocates subjects which include terms from the primary category.

c) Maintain an order of general before special within each category and sub-category.

d Maintain an order of general before special in the schedules of a classification scheme.

8 The notation of a library classification should be:

a) Irrelevant to the order.

b) The only factor determining the order.

c) Wholly subordinate to the order.

d) A minor factor in determining the order.

9 The index vocabulary of a classification scheme is:

a) The terms used in the alphabetical index.

b) The terms used in the schedules.

c) The notation.

d) The combination of terms used in the schedules and notation.

10 The combination order in an alphabetical list of subject headings:

a) May be the same as that used in a classification scheme.

b) Should never be the same as that used in a classification scheme.

c) Should be the reverse of that used in a classification scheme.

d) Should be worked out independently of that used in a classification scheme.

11 In an alphabetical list of subject headings instructions should

be included for the indexer to make *see also* references:

    a) *From* a selected term *towards* a related unused term.

    b) *Towards* a selected term *from* a related unused term.

    c) *From* a selected term *towards* a related used term.

    d) *Towards* a selected term *from* a related used term.

12 Oblique references are so called because they are made between:

    a) Terms which are only partly related.

    b) Terms which reflect a collateral relationship.

    c) Terms from different categories.

    d) Terms which reflect a hierarchical relationship.

13 In an alphabetical list of subject headings, and in a thesaurus, the approach vocabulary should be:

    a) Excluded.

    b) Included in a separate sequence.

    c) Included in a single sequence with the index vocabulary, but distinguished typographically.

    d) Included in a single sequence with the index vocabulary without any distinguishing mark.

14 A post-coordinate index language handles compound subjects by entering them in an index under:

    a) Single headings which comprise all the terms necessary to specify the subject.

    b) A series of headings, each comprising all the terms necessary to specify the subject, the order of terms being rotated.

    c) A series of headings, each comprising all the terms necessary to specify the subject, the order of terms being permutated.

    d) A series of headings, each comprising one of the terms necessary to specify the subject.

15 In a thesaurus a BT note indicates that, in relation to the term under which the note appears, the term following the note is:

    a) In the same category and super-ordinate.

    b) In the same category and subordinate.

    c) In a different category and super-ordinate.

    d) In a different category and subordinate

ANSWERS TO SELF TEST

1 (a) A structured index language is one which attempts to indicate relationships between terms.

2 (c) By literary warrant we mean that the initial choice of terms is based on a survey of the literature.

3 (c) Bachelors reflects the characteristics of *marital status* (single) and *sex* (male).

4 (a) In index language construction, subject analysis is the process by which we establish the categories to be recognized, and their scope.

5 (d) If a broad category includes a number of terms which are not mutually exclusive, we must proceed further with division to establish sub-categories. This is essential to ensure that we achieve predictability in indexing compound subjects.

6 (b) Combination order is the order in which terms are assembled to specify a compound subject.

7 (d) The principle of inversion must be observed if we wish to maintain an order of general before special in the schedules of a classification scheme.

8 (c) The notation of a library classification should be wholly subordinate to the order.

9 (c) The index vocabulary of a classification scheme is the notation.

10 (a) The combination order in an alphabetical list of subject headings may be the same as that used in a classification scheme.

11 (d) In an alphabetical list of subject headings instructions should be included for the indexer to make *see also* references *towards* a selected term *from* a related used term.

12 (c) Oblique references are so called because they are made between terms from different categories.

13 (c) In an alphabetical list of subject headings, and in a thesaurus, the approach vocabulary should be included in a single sequence with the index vocabulary, but distinguished typographically.

14 (d) A post-coordinate index language handles compound subjects by entering them in an index under a series of headings, each comprising one of the terms necessary to specify the subject.

15 (a) In a thesaurus a ʙᴛ note indicates that, in relation to the term under which the note appears, the term following the note is in the same category and super-ordinate.

RATING

9 or less: A less than satisfactory grasp of the essential points covered by the programme.

10-11: Satisfactory.

12-13: Good.

14-15: Excellent.